Leavenworth Papers

No. 5

*Fighting the Russians in Winter:
Three Case Studies*

by Dr. Allen F. Chew

Combat Studies Institute
U.S. Army Command and General Staff College
Fort Leavenworth, Kansas 66027

DECEMBER 1981

Contents

Maps v

Introduction vii

Chapter 1. Selected Examples and Lessons from the Undeclared Allied-Soviet War in Northern Russia During the Winter of 1918—19 1

Chapter 2. The Destruction of the Soviet 44th Motorized Rifle Division 17

Chapter 3. Pertinent Aspects of Nazi-Soviet Warfare During the Winter of 1941—42 31

Chapter 4. Conclusion 43

Notes 45

For sale by the Superintendent of Documents, U.S. Government Printing Office, Washington, D.C. 20402

Maps

1. Locale of Allied expedition to North Russia, 1918—19 3
2. Battle of Bolshie Ozerki, 31 March—2 April 1919 7
3. Soviet attack against Nizhnyaya Gora, 19 January 1919 11
4. Ninth Army objectives 19
5. General locale of Suomussalmi-Raate Campaign 22
6. Destruction of the 44th Division 27
7. The Soviet Winter Offensive, 1941—42 32

Introduction

The Russian winter defeated Napoleon, as every Frenchman knows. It also defeated Hitler, as most Germans know. Many Americans share that "knowledge"—which is false in both cases! Those popular myths illustrate the uncritical acceptance and perpetuation of rationalizations designed to obscure the fact that those "invincible" Western military paragons were humbled by the "inferior" Russians.

This paper will not discuss either of those ill-fated campaigns in detail. However, in regard to the claims of "General Winter," it should be noted that the main body of Napoleon's Grande Armée, initially at least 378,000 strong,[1] diminished by half during the first eight weeks of his invasion[2]—*before* the major battle of the campaign. This decrease was partly due to garrisoning supply centers, but disease, desertions, and casualties sustained in various minor actions caused thousands of losses.[3] At Borodino on 7 September 1812—the only major engagement fought in Russia—Napoleon could muster no more than 135,000 troops,[4] and he lost at least 30,000[5] of them to gain a narrow and Pyrrhic victory almost 600 miles deep in hostile territory. The sequels were his uncontested and self-defeating occupation of Moscow and his humiliating retreat, which began on 19 October, *before* the first severe frosts later that month[6] and the first snow on 5 November.[7]

Hitler's plans also miscarried *before* the onset of severe winter weather; he was so confident of a lightning victory that he did not prepare for even the possibility of winter warfare in Russia. Yet his eastern army suffered more than 734,000 casualties (about 23 percent of its average strength of 3,200,000 troops)[8] during the first five months of the invasion, and on 27 November 1941, General Eduard Wagner, the Quartermaster General of the German Army, reported that "We are at the end of our resources in both personnel and materiel. We are *about to be* confronted with the dangers of deep winter."[9] [My italics.]

Although the plans of both of those would-be conquerors of Russia failed before the arrival of winter, there is no denying that snow and severe frost contributed greatly to the magnitude of their *subsequent* problems and casualties. This study addresses those aspects of warfare in the vicinity of

European Russia. The harsh climate of that region can be an indiscriminate killer, and the successful army must adapt to winter conditions. In the following examples, all illustrating combat in northern and subarctic European Russia, both Russians and their opponents paid the ultimate price when they overlooked this reality.

Before turning to specific operations, it may be useful to list some of the pertinent environmental factors and their military ramifications. The obvious special conditions encountered in the northern latitudes are: extreme cold, deep snow, short days, and—in most subarctic locales—dense coniferous forests, sparse population (and consequently few ready-made shelters), and poor and widely separated roads. Their military corollaries are also readily apparent:

- Mobility and logistical support are restricted. Roads and runways can only be kept open by plowing or compacting the snow. Cross-country transport—if possible at all—requires wide-tracked vehicles or sleds.

- Infantrymen moving through deep snow rapidly become exhausted.

- Extended marches require skis or at least snowshoes.

- Without special lubricants firearms and motors may freeze up and become inoperative at subzero temperatures.

- Human efficiency and survival require adequate shelter. If not available locally, portable shelter must be provided.

- Frostbite* casualties may exceed battle losses unless troops wear proper clothing, including warm gloves and footgear.

- Speedy removal of the wounded from the battlefield to shelter is essential to prevent even minor wounds from resulting in death from exposure.[10]

In the following three case studies, examples drawn from recent history illustrate these and other distinctive aspects of winter warfare in the Russian environment.

ALLEN F. CHEW
Combat Studies Institute
U.S. Army Command and General
Staff College
Fort Leavenworth, Kansas

---

*Frostbite is damage resulting from low temperatures. Severe cases involve not only the skin and subcutaneous tissue but also deeper tissues, sometimes leading to gangrene and loss of affected parts. Persistent ischemia, secondary thrombosis, and livid cyanosis mark severe frostbite cases.

Selected Examples and Lessons From the Undeclared Allied-Soviet War in Northern Russia During the Winter of 1918–19

In 1918—19, thousands of Allied troops occupied the ports of Murmansk and Arkhangelsk and penetrated deep into the hinterland of northern Russia. This military operation was but one of a series of events that convulsed the Russian nation as a result of its involvement in World War I. In March 1917 the centuries-old czarist autocracy collapsed under the pressure of war, corruption, and social and economic dislocation. The inept Provisional Government that replaced the monarchy, plagued by internal strife and lacking popular support for its efforts to continue the disastrous war, fell easy prey to a Bolshevik military coup in November 1917. Four months later the Bolsheviks made good their well-publicized promise to remove Russia from the war by concluding a separate peace treaty with Germany. This "betrayal" caused considerable consternation among Russia's former allies. They feared that Germany might transfer hundreds of thousands of troops from Russia to the western front, where the war was still raging. Also cause for alarm was the possibility that Allied war materiel in Russia might fall into German hands or be used by the Bolsheviks—who espoused the violent eradication of the existing international order—to consolidate their hold on the country. Faced with these and other grim prospects, the Allied Supreme War Council decided in 1918 to send military units into northern Russia and eastern Siberia.

The misadventure in northern Russia, with which this chapter is concerned, began when about 150 British marines landed at Murmansk in early March 1918. At the beginning of August about 1,200 French troops, British marines, and American sailors debarked at Arkhangelsk. The ostensible reason for the Allied landings was to prevent German seizure of the vast stores of war materiel accumulated at those ports, but after the Armistice between the Allies and the Central Powers on 11 November 1918 that pretext lost all validity. At that time there were more then 13,000 Allied troops stationed along the Murmansk Railroad and about 11,000 scattered in an irregular semicircle radiating from Arkhangelsk. Attempts to expel the Bolsheviks from Arkhangelsk province had stalled in the fall of 1918, and with the onset of winter, Allied commanders were concerned primarily with holding defensive positions while awaiting the outcome of the political debate over the future course of the intervention. That debate ended in the spring of 1919. Unable to agree among themselves on the ultimate purpose of the intervention, and faced with vocal opposition from their constituents and declining morale among their troops, Western leaders decided to withdraw their forces from northern Russia. The withdrawal began in June and July when the Americans left Arkhangelsk, and ended in October when the last British troops departed from Murmansk.[1]

The diplomatic complexities of this poorly conceived and ill-fated intervention are beyond the scope of this paper. Suffice it to say that Allied motives concerning the North Russian Expedition were varied, confused, and sometimes contradictory. What is important for the purpose of this study is that Allied troops, including about five thousand Americans,[2] were involved in combat with the nascent Red Army.

The Allied forces based at Murmansk and at Arkhangelsk comprised separate fronts, commanded by the British Major Generals C. M. Maynard and William Edmund Ironside. Because the Arkhangelsk district witnessed more fighting than the Murmansk hinterland during the winter of 1918—19, the following examples are from the Arkhangelsk region. General Ironside assumed command of the Allied forces on the Arkhangelsk front in the fall of 1918. Within his small command, the order of battle was extremely complex. In addition to the U.S. 339th Infantry Regiment (with supporting engineer and medical units), there were about 6,000 British troops, 500 Canadian field artillerymen, 900—1,700 French soldiers, plus small numbers (only about 500 in the aggregate) of Poles, Italians, Estonians, Lithuanians, Czechs, Serbs, Finns, and Chinese. Not included in the figure of 11,000 cited above were various Russian contingents which fluctuated widely in both numbers and reliability—including a small unit of the French Foreign Legion and a larger Slavo-British Legion.[3]

Opposing Ironside's polyglot forces were the Bolshevik troops of Comdr. Aleksandr A. Samoilo's Sixth Independent Army, which probably had no more than 14,000 combat effectives during that winter's fighting. Although they were a more homogeneous force than the Allies, they included a Chinese company and a Finnish regiment.[4]

In the campaigns fought during the winter of 1918—19, each side at times displayed sound adaptation to climatic challenges and at other times made fatal mistakes. The Red Army suffered far heavier casualties than the Americans (and other Allied units) partly because of the different postures of the two forces: U.S. troops were generally on the defensive during the winter, whereas the Soviets mounted nearly continuous raids[5] and several determined offensives. A well-sheltered defender enjoyed a marked advantage over his exposed attacker advancing through deep snow in subzero cold. Ironside recognized this fundamental fact. After a few limited and abortive attacks designed to secure more advantageous winter outposts, he concentrated on the defense of his far-flung positions.[6] Stressing the impor-

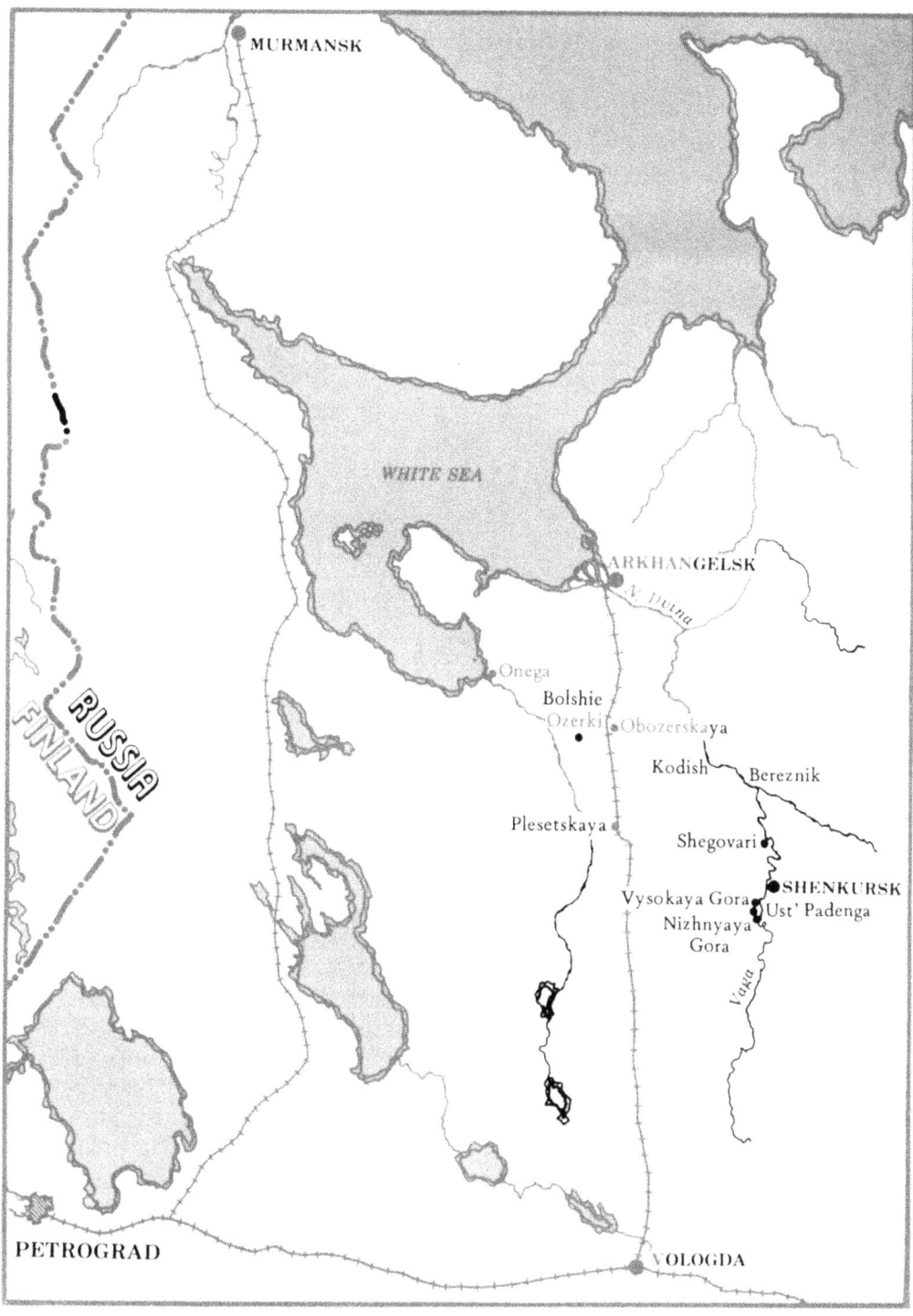

Map 1. Locale of Allied expedition to North Russia, 1918—19.

tance of shelter in those conditions,* Ironside noted that any attack had to be short in duration and, as its ultimate objective, had to secure cover.[7]

American outpost, Northern Russia, 1918—19

The most costly battles of the North Russian campaign, fought near Bolshie Ozerki from 31 March to 2 April 1919,[8] clearly illustrate the advantages of the defense.

The tiny village of Bolshie Ozerki lay between the port of Onega and the important Allied position at Obozerskaya Station on the Arkhangelsk-Vologda railroad. Because the port at the main Allied base of Arkhangelsk was frozen fast during the winter, any reinforcements for the railroad front had to travel overland from the distant ice-free port at Murmansk via the minor road through Bolshie Ozerki. When the 6th Yorkshire Regiment was dispatched over this arduous route towards the end of winter, the Red command decided to seize Bolshie Ozerki to prevent those troops from linking up with the Allied forces at Obozerskaya.[9]

---

*Shelter not only provided warmth, which benefited both men and weapons, but also concealed the defenders. The attackers, silhouetted against the snow and leaving revealing tracks, were easily spotted. Even when they wore white capes, their faces and weapons were visible. The attackers also suffered exhaustion from moving through the heavy snow.

The preliminaries to the major engagements at the end of the month began on 17 March, when a ski detachment of Red partisans led by Osip Palkin reconnoitered the village's defenses undetected, quietly captured two sentries, and learned the precise locations of the Allied positions. With this intelligence, Comdr. Petr A. Solodukhin's brigade of 600 to 800 men surprised and overwhelmed the garrison of 80 to 160 French and White Russian troops[10] and captured the outpost at Bolshie Ozerki intact.[11]

A small-scale Allied counterattack from Obozerskaya the next day proved abortive,[12] but it probably contributed to the Soviet decision to suspend temporarily all offensive operations. The Sixth Army commander, former czarist Maj. Gen. A. A. Samoilo, issued that order to his entire field staff on 18 March. He cited these factors in the decision: shortages of warm footgear and other provisions; the perilous situation of Solodukhin's column (which, according to Samoilo's information, had not succeeded in capturing all of the buildings of the village); and Comdr. Ieronim P. Uborevich's report that on another Sixth Army sector half of the troops of his attacking battalions had either frozen to death or been disabled by frostbite when the temperature dropped below -30°C (-22°F).[13]

When Samoilo issued an order on 19 March to resume operations on 25 March—with Obozerskaya now the main objective—the commander in chief of the Red Army, the former czarist Col. Ioakim I. Vatsetis, countermanded it "because of the severe frost."[14]

On 23 March about 320 men of the 6th Yorkshire Regiment and 70 Americans from Company H, 339th Infantry Regiment, launched coordinated attacks on Bolshie Ozerki from positions west of the village. They soon became exhausted, however, from wading through waist-deep snow, which also ruled out a charge. Under heavy machine gun fire, they had to abandon the attack.[15]

A simultaneous assault on the eastern approaches to the village fared no better. About 300 White Russian and 40 to 80 British troops were halted along the roadway by effective enemy fire. At that point, Company E, 339th Infantry, tried to flank the Red defenses by skirting through the woods north of the road. Already tired from a ten-mile march in their awkward Shackleton boots,* the soldiers of Company E required about four hours to cover less than three miles, whereupon they were recalled to their starting point. The Allies lost about seventy-five men in those two futile attacks.[16] After that failure, Ironside, who had recently taken personal command in that sector, decided to destroy the village by artillery fire, which was largely accomplished on 25 March, just before he returned to Arkhangelsk.[17]

---

*That canvas-and-leather footgear had been designed by the famous Antarctic explorer, Sir Ernest Shackleton. Although warm and adequate for sedentary use or with skis, their smooth soles and low heels made them extremely slippery on ice or packed snow; Ironside considered the natives' felt boot superior. (Halliday, p. 148; Ironside, p. 63)

Despite the weather, both sides continued to bring up reinforcements for the impending showdown. The Allies constructed strong wooden blockhouses, log barricades, and troop shelters about four miles east of the village, on the road to Obozerskaya some twelve miles farther east. By the end of the month they had pulled up from their railroad positions all available artillery, mainly 75-mm guns manned by White Russians. They also concentrated all the troops they could spare from Arkhangelsk and other sectors, including Companies E, I, and M of the U.S. 339th Infantry, three infantry companies and one machine gun company of White Russians, two Yorkshire platoons, and an invaluable section of the U.S. 310th Engineers.[18]

Those Allied forces, totaling less than 2,000 men,[19] were opposed by an estimated 7,000 Red troops,[20] including (among other units not positively identified) the 2d Moscow Regiment,[21] the 97th Saratov Regiment,[22] and a brigade from Kamyshin (possibly part of Commander Kuznetsov's Kamyshinsk Division).[23] The Soviet artillery included a battery of 4.2-inch guns that had been hauled about thirty-seven miles over a minor road at the cost of uncounted dead horses.[24]

About 0830 on 31 March the Reds cut the phone lines between Obozerskaya and the road positions, and later in the morning three battalions of the 2d Moscow Regiment flanked the Allies on the north and attempted to capture two 75-mm guns from the rear. Lieutenant Lukovsky, the White Russian in charge of those pieces, reversed them in time to get off four rounds of shrapnel at point-blank range. His action, coupled with the effective fire of Corporal Pratt's Lewis gun* team (Company M, 339th Infantry), halted the attack with heavy losses to the Muscovites. Thereafter the fighting shifted to the frontal positions, where the Reds launched repeated attacks from the direction of Bolshie Ozerki throughout the day. All failed under the devastating fire from the forward blockhouse and the frontline posts, and Allied artillery took an added toll of the enemy until darkness brought a lull in the battle.

The main Soviet effort began on 1 April about 0330 (shortly after daybreak) with determined frontal attacks and a weaker demonstration in the rear. Inflicting heavy losses, the defenders drove back these and all subsequent attacks with the same effective machine gun, rifle, and artillery fire.[25] At times they even used rifle grenades when the attackers came within their 200-yard range.[26]

Several deserters who crossed the lines intermittently on that April Fool's Day revealed demoralization within the Red units; they reported that an entire company of the 97th Saratov Regiment had refused to advance.[27]

---

*The Lewis gun was a gas-operated, air-cooled light machine gun with a horizontal drum magazine which held 47 rounds of .30-inch caliber ammunition; its rate of fire was about 500 rounds per minute.

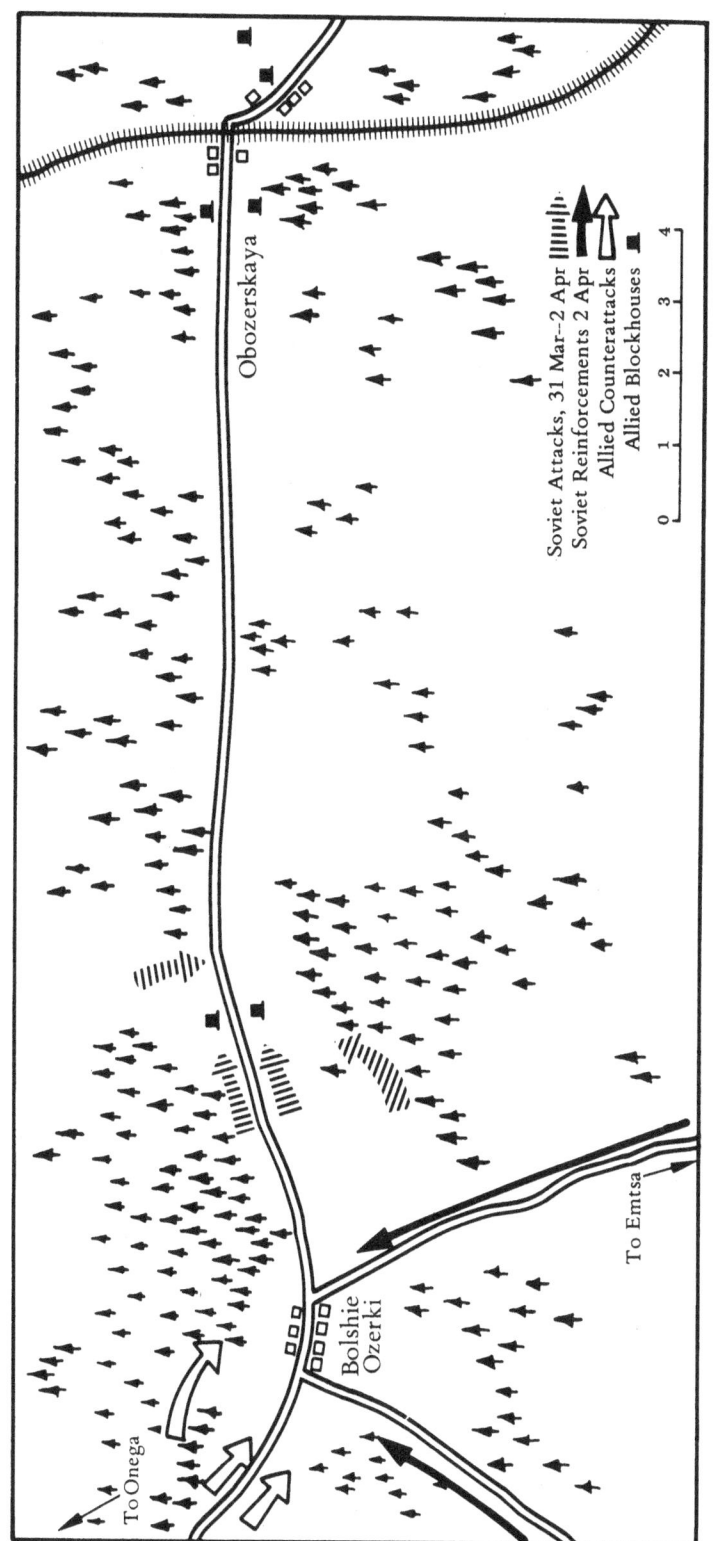

Map 2. Battle of Bolshie Ozerki, 31 March – 2 April 1919.

Nevertheless, because the Allies were still outnumbered and because the fighting was so protracted and intense, the Allied command ordered a diversionary attack on Bolshie Ozerki from the west to relieve the pressure on the units so heavily engaged east of that village.

As envisioned in the operations order for the diversionary blow, Company C of the 6th Yorkshire Regiment, commanded by Lieutenant Marsh, would move along a trail through the woods to flank the village from the north. A White Russian officer had recently reconnoitered the trail, and Lieutenant Marsh had Russian guides. Captain Bailey's Company A (Yorkshires) would advance along another trail made about a week earlier; a detachment moving along the main road leading into the village from the northwest would protect its right flank. Bailey would be assisted by an American trench mortar detachment and a machine gun team from Company H, 339th Infantry, which would also provide two infantry platoons for the reserve. Part of a White Russian machine gun company would also support the two Yorkshire companies. A company of Polish troops was to advance along the main road and to deploy south of the roadway upon enemy contact.[28]

This counterblow, however, was no more successful than the Soviet offensive that continued at the same time. The Allies had fixed zero hour for 0300 on 2 April, but at 0200 Lieutenant Marsh reported that his company was lost in the woods, that his horses were belly-deep in the snow, and that he could not proceed. Thus one of the main elements in the attack was neutralized until it returned to the main road, far from its objective, about 0510. By then the Poles had suffered heavily and had retired from the battle temporarily. By 0610 Company A was partially surrounded and forced to yield ground. Captain Bailey was killed about this time, and his successor, Lieutenant Goodloss, ordered a withdrawal. Lt. Clifford Phillips's platoon (Company H, 339th Infantry) rushed up from the reserves to cover the British pullback.[29] In the subsequent delaying action, that American officer was also mortally wounded.[30]

The remainder of the day witnessed mostly artillery and mortar exchanges, until Red pressure on both flanks provoked a successful Allied counterattack about 1730. The Reds disengaged around 1900, and about an hour later the Allies began withdrawing under the cover of darkness to their quarters at settlements in the rear. By then they were suffering from exhaustion, and there were many cases of severe frostbite.[31]

Soviet operations at the road position east of Bolshie Ozerki had resumed on 2 April with an exceptionally heavy artillery and mortar barrage, answered by an effective counterbarrage. Only weak infantry attacks were attempted, however, and even they petered out by noon. The costs of the previous attacks apparently decided the issue: there were no more attacks after 2 April,[32] and by the fifth the Reds were withdrawing from the area.

Further delay would have risked the loss, or at least prolonged immobilization, of their guns and sleighs in the spring mud.[33] Those fierce engagements at the turn of the month were the last major battles of the campaign in northern Russia. The Soviet forces had been temporarily checked, and the Allies began to evacuate as soon as Arkhangelsk was reopened to navigation.

In the battles around Bolshie Ozerki, the *defense* won both of the main rounds: the Allies defended their road positions, and the Reds defended Bolshie Ozerki. Both attacking forces suffered heavy casualties from exposure to the weather, although the days were sunny and the nighttime temperatures by then were no worse than a relatively mild -20°C (-4°F).[34] By day the sunshine melted the snow, which soaked through the canvas tops of the Shackleton boots and caused more cases of frostbite among the Allied troops than they had experienced during the coldest days of winter[35] when temperatures sometimes dropped below -40°.* Their enemies suffered even heavier losses; a Soviet source acknowledges more than 500 frostbite casualties in the brigade from Kamyshin alone.[36] In view of that, Allied estimates of 2,000 Red casualties from all sources may have erred on the conservative side.[37]

One reason for those excessive Soviet losses was that the Red command recklessly committed the brigade that arrived from the milder climate of the southern Volga before it could receive proper clothing; it had neither the felt boots (*valenki*) nor the sheepskin coats issued to other Sixth Army units.[38] Nevertheless, the mere fact that thousands of Soviet troops were deployed in the open for days on end doomed many to freeze to death or to suffer frostbite.

The operations near Shenkursk in January 1919 provided examples of other pertinent problems. Having occupied that imposing district center of several thousand inhabitants in September,[39] the Allies had had time to fortify it strongly. When the crisis described below developed in January, the Allies had sufficient provisions to last two months, and the garrison—counting the outposts in nearby villages—totaled about 1,700 American, British, Canadian, and White Russian troops.[40] They undoubtedly could have taken a terrible toll of any force attacking them in winter. The town, however, was situated on the frozen Vaga River more than 200 miles southeast of Arkhangelsk, far in advance of any Allied positions on either flank,[41] and therefore highly vulnerable to encirclement. General Ironside ordered the local commander, Colonel Graham, to evacuate at once if the enemy attempted an enveloping movement.[42]

---

*-40°C = -40°F

Commander Samoilo had in mind just such an operation, one intended not only to destroy the Shenkursk garrison, but also to seize the mouth of the Vaga north of the town.[43] He made elaborate preparations for the offensive, deploying at least 3,100 infantry[44] for coordinated attacks from three directions. The supporting artillery included several 4.2-inch howitzers[45] and one 6-inch gun.[46] A detachment of about 150 local partisans was detailed to strike at Shegovari, a village some twenty-five road miles to the rear (north) of Shenkursk, held by about ninety Americans.[47] Two other partisan units of similar size were to reconnoiter, harass the enemy flanks, select populated points along the march routes, and stock them in advance with provisions, fodder, and medicine.[48] Although white camouflage coveralls were not available, some of the units prepared for surprise attacks by removing their sheepskin coats and substituting quilted trousers and jackets, over which they wore long white peasant shirts and white pants. Thus blending into the snowy landscape, they could not be detected beyond 50—125 feet.[49]

The largest of the three main detachments, led by future Soviet Lieutenant General Filippovsky, consisted of more than 1,300 infantrymen,[50] six heavy guns,[51] and twenty-one machine guns.[52] Assigned the task of a frontal assault, it bore the brunt of the actual fighting,[53] which took place primarily at the outposts south of Shenkursk. Nizhnyaya Gora, farthest from the town—about fifteen miles—was hit first and hardest. The only troops there when Samoilo's massive blow fell were the forty-seven men of the 4th Platoon of Company A, 339th Regiment, and even that small unit was divided: Lt. Harry Mead had twenty-two men at the exposed southern point, and a sergeant was in charge of twenty-three others at the other end of the village. To the left rear, a company of Cossacks held the neighboring village of Ust'Padenga. About a mile farther to the rear, at Vysokaya Gora, the remainder of Captain Odjard's Company A manned five sturdy blockhouses on a commanding bluff, supported by two light guns which were serviced alternately by Canadian and White Russian gunners. In all three villages Captain Odjard had a total of 450 riflemen, eighteen machine guns, and two artillery pieces.[54]

Early on the morning of 19 January, when the mercury hit -36°C (-33°F),[55] Filippovsky's powerful guns shook Nizhnyaya Gora from positions beyond the range of the smaller Allied pieces.[56] From their tiny outpost Lieutenant Mead's half platoon saw far across the frozen Vaga River hundreds of dark figures advancing slowly through powder snow, which varied in depth from three to more than four feet.[57] Just before they came within small-arms range, the barrage lifted, and the Americans were stunned by the sudden appearance of about 100 to 150 ghostly white-clad figures[58] who rushed them on three sides from nearby snowdrifts into which they had crept undetected before dawn. Within seconds a bitter fight was underway, and the Allied machine guns tore into the attackers with great effect.

But Mead's hopelessly outnumbered men were also taking losses, and he ordered a hasty retreat. When the survivors joined the remainder of the

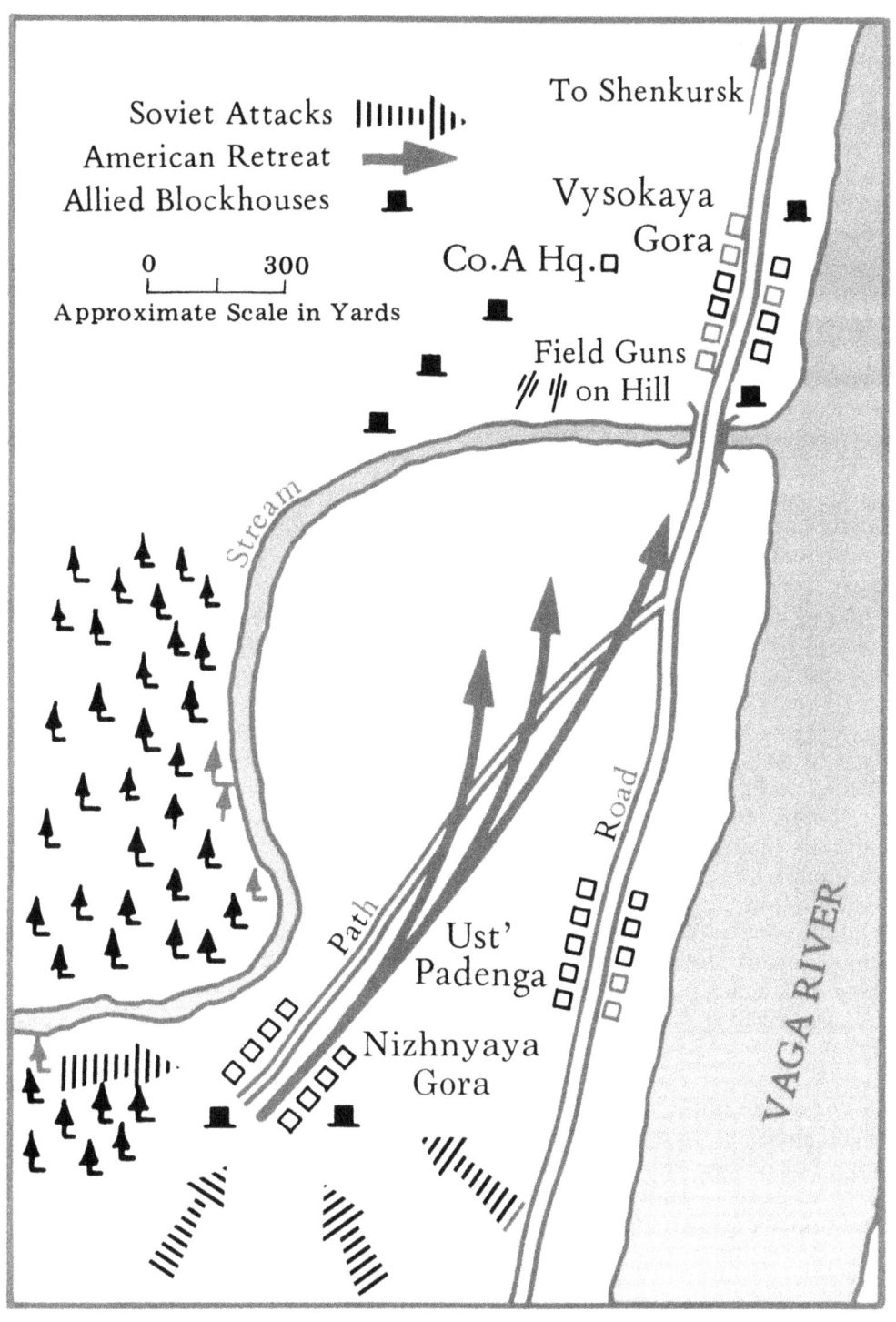

Map 3. Soviet attack against Nizhnyaya Gora, 19 January 1919.

platoon at the rear of the village, they faced a terrible prospect: their only route to the security of Vysokaya Gora lay down a hill, across a valley 800 yards wide, and up another hill to the friendly blockhouses—the entire distance through deep snow with no protective cover. As they struggled through the snow drifts, they made perfect targets, and only seven of the platoon's original forty-seven members made it unscathed to friendly shelter.[59] The Reds had lost an estimated 150 men,[60] and the hundreds who swarmed into Nizhnyaya Gora were no doubt exhausted from their own long march through the snow; consequently, there was no determined pursuit on that day. Filippovsky seemed content for the moment to wear down the defenders with his artillery, which fired about 1,000 rounds on the nineteenth and 800 the next day.[61] The Cossack company at Ust'Padenga departed under the cover of darkness and reached Vysokaya Gora undetected on the night of the nineteenth.[62]

From 20 to 22 January it was the Reds' turn to face the ordeal of crossing the open valley below Vysokaya Gora. Canadian gunners, firing shrapnel from their commanding positions on the hilltop, slaughtered the Soviet infantry struggling through the snow below them. A Soviet source acknowledges that one of the Red battalions lost half its men in those unsuccessful attacks.[63] The Allied defenses stood firm, but on the evening of 22 January Colonel Graham ordered Captain Odjard to retire on Shenkursk, because it had become obvious that the town was the main Red objective.[64]

Odjard's weary troops had scarcely reached Shenkursk, late in the afternoon of 24 January, when Colonel Graham decided to evacuate that town without a fight, in compliance with General Ironside's standing order. The day before, the partisan raid had been carried out at Shegovari, and reconnaissance had revealed that Soviet forces held nearly all of the roads from Shenkursk. Enemy artillery was shelling the town from the northwest, the northeast, and the south,[65] and communications to the rear were severed in the afternoon.[66] A successful withdrawal was already problematical; to remain longer meant slow but nearly certain annihilation. In fact, by midnight all three of Samoilo's main columns were in their designated positions in nearby villages, ready to begin a coordinated attack on the morning of the twenty-fifth.[67]

The escape of the entire Allied force, approximately 1,500 troops accompanied by about 500 civilians, was due to a combination of intelligent leadership, strict march discipline, and sheer luck. In silent but determined flight during the night of 24–25 January, the evacuating column followed a little-used winter trail that the Reds had overlooked.[68]

Lt. Hugh McPhail of Company A ingeniously ordered his platoon to cut off their cumbersome overcoats at knee length, a precaution for which they were thankful on the long and difficult march that covered thirty-five to forty miles in two days.[69] The awkward Shackleton boots, however, caused more trouble. After struggling along precariously on the icy trail that night, many soldiers discarded those boots and continued in stocking feet—which led to disabling frostbite.[70]

Shenkursk was an important psychological and tactical victory for the Sixth Army, but Commander Samoilo acknowledged that it failed in two of its main objectives: it did not destroy the Allied garrison or capture the mouth of the Vaga River.[71] Among the causes for those disappointments enumerated by his military commissar, Nikolai N. Kuzmin, was the fact that the attackers did not pursue aggressively because, after twelve days of slim rations and exposure to severe frost, the comforts and vast stores of provisions at Shenkursk proved irresistible.[72] Samoilo also noted that this operation served as a school for his troops, especially by demonstrating the need for ski training.[73]

Although a detailed description of all the Allied positions and local engagements is impractical, certain additional aspects of the campaign in northern Russia warrant attention for their technical lessons. At Obozerskaya Allied troops lived in 257 converted railroad boxcars. (The same improvised shelters were used at Murmansk.) Remodeled, insulated, and heated with small sheet-iron stoves, they were warm and comfortable,[74] although one veteran of the expeditionary force remarked that they were "most unhygienic."[75]

Both sides recognized the value of skis, but neither had enough troops trained to use them. For example, a Soviet ski battalion from Vyatka (modern Kirov), destined for and needed by the Sixth Army, had to be assigned instead to the Third Army.[76] The British employed a Finnish officer to train Company D of the 6th Yorkshire Regiment as a mobile ski column; however, in its first three weeks of combat, it suffered 160 cases of frostbite (compared to only eighteen battle casualties).[77]

Snowshoes were also used on occasion, but a major Allied experiment with them proved a disappointment. Captain Barbateau, an experienced French Canadian woodsman, ordered several thousand pairs of appropriate snowshoes from Canada, but they were shipped to Murmansk instead of Arkhangelsk. He therefore had to use the "bear paw" type issued by British Ordnance. Oval hoops about eighteen inches long, they were too small to support a man's weight in the dry and powdery snow of the northern Russian winter. He nevertheless trained several platoons of White Russians to use them and proudly dubbed his detachment "Les Coureurs de Bois." Their first combat mission was a flank attack on Emtsa in December, as part of a larger operation designed to capture Plesetskaya. Floundering in the deep snow in the woods, his men covered only a kilometer or so an hour. During the first day they progressed only about six miles—less than halfway to their objective. Even then they were so exhausted that Barbateau requested a two-day rest before proceeding, and the whole operation was called off before his detachment could engage the enemy.[78]

The extreme cold caused many weapons to become inoperative. Lt. John Baker (of the 339th Infantry) reported an engagement on 30 December during which all of his Lewis guns were either frozen or broken.[79] In an operation on 5 December, a strong Allied detachment was preparing to attack a superior Red force northeast of Shenkursk. The Allies narrowly escaped disaster when, just before the scheduled assault, they learned that neither the automatic cannon nor the Vickers* machine guns were working because their oil had frozen. This discovery occurred barely in time to permit a successful retreat.[80]

The Ford trucks used by the Allied expedition in northern Russia proved unreliable in the severe cold and deep snow, for even packed trails required the continuous use of low gear. General Ironside wisely chose to travel by the common native sleigh. Those simple but practical conveyances, pulled by small but rugged ponies that could survive in the open when necessary, were the backbone of the logistics of both sides.[81]

American supply column, Arkhangelsk region, January 1919

---

*The Vickers was a water-cooled, recoil-operated, tripod-mounted medium machine gun fed by a fabric belt holding 250 rounds of .303-inch caliber ammunition; its rate of fire was about 500 rounds per minute.

The special aspects of winter warfare illustrated by this chapter may be summarized briefly:

• The defensive was normally superior to the offensive because the attacker had to contend with debilitating exposure to frost and wind chill, exhaustion from moving through deep snow, relative lack of concealment, longer exposure to enemy fire because rushing was not feasible, and aggravated supply problems. Any offensive had to be limited in both time and distance—and had to have prospects of securing shelter.

• Troops not acclimated to the harsh environment had less chance for survival. Appropriate clothes and boots were essential, and their use required supervision: long overcoats were not practical for long marches; camouflage required white outer garments.

• The wrong snowshoes were virtually useless.

• The value of trained ski troops was underscored by their scarcity on both sides.

• The lack of special lubricants caused weapons to freeze at critical moments. Motor vehicles also proved unreliable, and native horse sleighs provided the most dependable transport.

• The climate compounded distances, for all deployments and maneuvers, especially cross-country movements, required extra time.

• Deep snow and ice complicated both retreat and pursuit. Where they had to cover open terrain in those operations, both sides found themselves in highly vulnerable positions.

Both contestants knew—or rapidly learned—those principles of winter combat, and under ideal conditions both practiced them. That they violated those sound concepts so frequently in practice—with generally fatal consequences—was most often because both sides were operating on a shoestring. The Allies could not substantially reinforce or re-equip their small forces because their main base was icebound, and the Soviet command—simultaneously faced with much greater perils on other fronts—could not spare more resources for its Sixth Army.[82]

The Destruction of the Soviet 44th Motorized Rifle Division[1]

On 30 November 1939 the Red Army invaded Finland without a declaration of war and achieved tactical surprise at numerous points along the 900-mile common border. Despite their overwhelming odds in men and firepower and their virtual monopoly of armor, Soviet forces suffered severe and humiliating reverses during the first several weeks of that 105-day conflict. A partial explanation is that about a third of Finland is north of the Arctic Circle, where one of the coldest winters on record had already begun. The Finns were prepared for combat in snow at subzero temperatures; the invaders were not. It was almost that simple.

Not all Red Army commanders, however, were indifferent to environmental factors or ignorant of Finnish capabilities. An eighty-seven-page pamphlet, *Finlandiya i ee Armiya* [Finland and its army], published by the Soviet Commissariat of Defense in 1937, noted that all Finnish troops were experienced skiers trained for winter warfare, and that their field exercises emphasized Finland's many natural defenses: rivers, swamps, thousands of lakes, and vast forests. The future marshal of the Soviet Union, Kirill Meretskov, then commander of the Leningrad Military District, which was initially responsible for the entire Soviet operation, cautioned on the eve of the invasion that serious resistance could be expected. Comdr. Boris Shaposhnikov, Chief of the General Staff of the Red Army, also anticipated a lengthy struggle against stubborn defenders.

On the mistaken assumption that Finnish workers would welcome the Red Army as liberators, Stalin ignored his military advisers and rushed into the invasion without adequate preparation. In 1939—as in June of 1941—the Soviet military services paid an enormous price for Stalin's political miscalculations.

The most dramatic illustration of the price the Finns extracted was their annihilation of the 44th Motorized Rifle Division in January 1940. That battle is a classic example of what well-trained and appropriately equipped troops can accomplish against an enemy who has superiority in numbers and firepower but is not prepared for the special conditions of a subarctic environment. Such a region typically has dense coniferous forests, few and widely separated roads, and a very cold climate—not a favorable setting for the deployment of standard motorized or armored units in winter. It is a realm where specially trained and equipped light infantry may prove its worth.

Among the four Soviet armies initially involved in the invasion, the Ninth Army was to bisect Finland at its narrow waist by driving for the northern end of the Gulf of Bothnia. On 30 November the Ninth Army commander hurled three divisions across the border, but they could not cooperate with one another because they were separated by sixty to one hundred miles of roadless woods. Thus it is possible to examine the central prong of the Ninth Army's offensive in isolation from other operations.

The main units of the 163d Rifle Division brushed aside a fifty-man covering detachment on the minor road that ran from the border near Juntusranta to Suomussalmi village, while the division's reconnaissance battalion and one rifle regiment pushed back two Finnish infantry battalions along the better road to Suomussalmi from Raate, about thirty miles south of Juntusranta. On 7 December the two columns joined forces to capture Suomussalmi, some twenty-five miles from the Soviet border. There a brigade of less than 5,000 men held the 163d Division in check until more reinforcements could reach that remote district.

By Christmas the Finnish forces totaled 11,500 men, reorganized as the 9th Division. This division had been formed in haste from various reserve units that happened to be available; only one of its three infantry regiments, JR*27, commanded by Lt. Col. Johan Mäkiniemi, had been a part of that division before the war (the other peacetime regiments had previously been deployed to distant regions). Lt. Col. Karl Mandelin's newly formed JR65 was rushed to Suomussalmi from Oulu. Lt. Col. Frans Fagernäs's JR64 arrived from the southwest and included the only regular army troops in the division. These reserve units had never before served together, but coordination was good because all of the regimental commanders and the division commander, Col. Hjalmar Siilasvuo, were veterans of the 27th Jäger Battalion. That unit of some 1,800 Finnish volunteers had fought in the Kaiser's army against the Russians in the First World War. After Finland gained its independence from Russia in December 1917, those Jäger veterans received additional battle experience in the Finnish civil war of 1918. They aslo became the nucleus of the Finnish officer corps.

On 27 December Colonel Siilasvuo launched a major counterattack against his opponent, who outnumbered him by several thousand men and also enjoyed a vast superiority in firepower. In two days of fierce fighting the Finns shattered the 163d Division; before the month ended its survivors

---

*JR: infantry regiment.

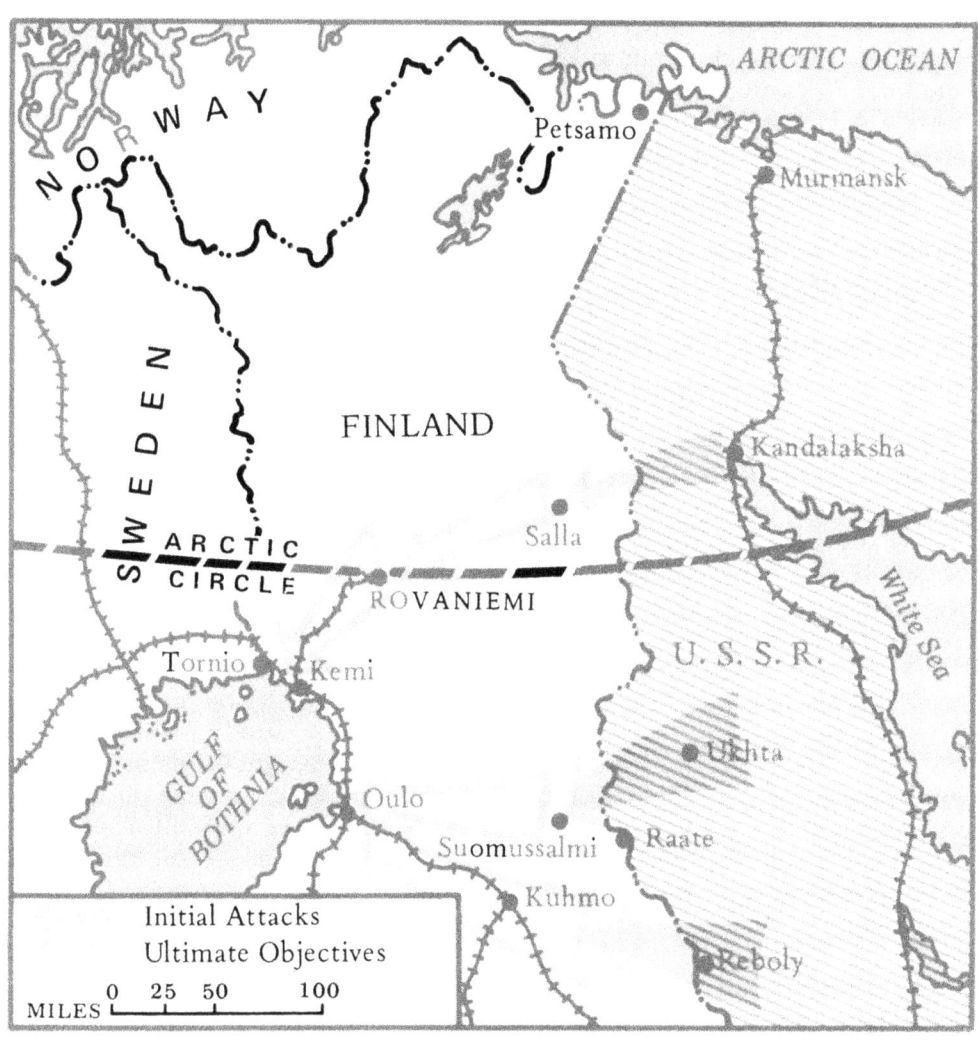

Map 4. Ninth Army objectives.

were fleeing in disorder northeast towards the frontier. By then the snow was at least three feet deep and the mercury dipped to -30° to -40°. Daylight lasted only about five hours.

While the battle with the 163d Division was still developing, the Ninth Army had dispatched along the Raate road a strong reinforcement, Commander Vinogradov's elite 44th Motorized Rifle Division. This regular army unit was originally from the Kiev Military District, and most of its troops were Ukrainians who were not familiar with northern woods. (In contrast, many of Siilasvuo's men were lumberjacks in peacetime.) The crew of the Finns' lone airplane* spotted advance elements of the 44th Motorized Infantry Division as early as 13 December, and they estimated that the main components were on the Raate road by the twenty-fourth. Had they succeeded in linking up with the 163d Division in time, the defense of central Finland would have been seriously jeopardized.

However, Colonel Siilasvuo had countered this potential threat before it became a reality. On 11 December he established a roadblock at a ridge between Lakes Kuivasjärvi and Kuomasjärvi, about six miles southeast of Suomussalmi. There Capt. Simo Makinen's two infantry companies, reinforced by additional mortars and guns, held up the advance of the entire 44th Division. Their success was due both to their own initiative and mobility and to the fact that the road-bound Russians were vulnerably ignorant about the strength and dispositions of the Finns.

The 44th Division had large amounts of motorized equipment, including about fifty tanks, all of which were confined to a single narrow dirt road through a pine forest. Under those circumstances the division could not bring more than a fraction of its abundant firepower to bear on the Finns at the roadblock. Although they had several hundred pairs of skis, none of the Russians had been trained to use them; therefore, even the infantry was confined to a radius of a few hundred yards on either side of the roadway.

In contrast, all of the Finns were experienced skiers and thus able to keep the 44th Division under constant surveillance. They also harassed it night and day with hit-and-run attacks on both of its vulnerable flanks, which stretched nearly twenty miles from the roadblock to the border. Approaching silently on skis and camouflaged in their white snowsuits, the

---

*Colonel Siilasvuo had but one obsolete plane at his disposal. Although it could be flown only at dawn or dusk, it was effective for reconnaissance because the Russians were clearly visible on the roads. The Soviets employed very few aircraft here, although the Finns saw many bombers overhead enroute to Oulu and other rear areas. Because of short days and the cover provided by the dense forests, air power played a very minor role in the early campaigns in central Finland in general. The Soviets then directed their bombing efforts mainly against Finnish towns and the defenses on the Karelian Isthmus far to the south.

Finnish raiders often achieved complete surprise. When they opened fire from the woods at close range, their Suomi submachine guns (firing seventy rounds per magazine) were especially effective.*

Misled by the frequency and effectiveness of those attacks, Commander Vinogradov believed that a much larger force opposed him. Consequently, he made no major effort to rescue the 163d Division while it was being destroyed just six to eight miles beyond the roadblock. The minor attacks he launched on 24 and 25 December failed to dislodge Captain Makinen's small force. On the twenty-seventh, Vinogradov scheduled a new attempt to smash the roadblock for 1030 the next morning, but raids by two Finnish companies early on 28 December led him to revoke that order and to direct his division to dig in for defense on the road.

While still preoccupied with the numerically superior 163d Division, Siilasvuo had the foresight to order the preparation of an improvised winter road for future operations against the 44th Division. A truck equipped with a snow plow was driven over a series of frozen lakes that paralleled the Raate road about four to six miles to the south to form the winter road. The Finns also began clearing a snow trail about fifteen miles long from Moisiovaara, at the end of an existing road, to the winter road (the so-called ice road). This road system enabled them to supply their forces on the enemy's southern flank from a railhead twenty miles beyond Moisiovaara.

The Finns plowed another improvised road along the Haukipera watercourse to a point just west of Lake Kuivasjärvi. From there the road went overland (out of sight of the Russians across that lake near the roadblock), skirted the lake on the south, and then turned east. Where these winter roads branched cross-country from watercourses, the Finns used their usual method of compacting snow in areas where truck plows were impractical: a skier led a horse through the snow (in deep snow the horse proceeded by a series of jumps, which necessitated the rotation of lead animals), followed by a horse pulling an empty sled, followed in turn by a series of horse-drawn sleds with progressively heavier loads.

Previous Finnish experience in bitter fighting just north of Lake Ladoga had indicated that three miles was the extreme limit for effective flanking attacks in wooded wilderness. More ambitious attempts had failed because of the problems of communications, supply, and artillery control in such a heavily forested environment. Thanks to Siilasvuo's winter roads, however, which alleviated those problems, large-scale flanking attacks were successful fifteen miles beyond the roadblock.

---

*Each Finnish division was authorized 250 of these weapons, ideal for forest fighting which is necessarily at close range. The Russian forces in Finland had nothing similar until February 1940.

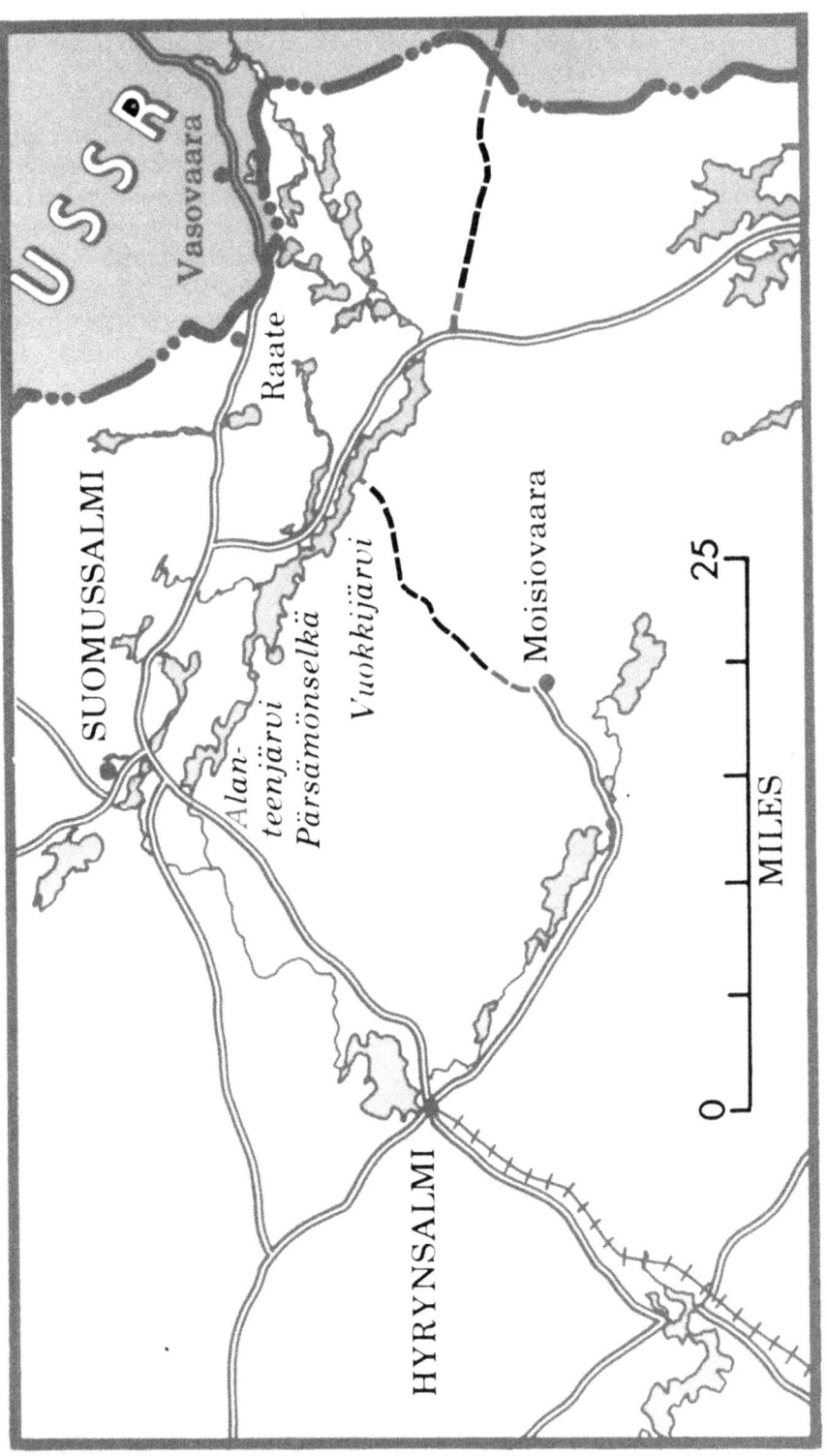

Map 5. General locale of Suomussalmi-Raate Campaign.

The initial moves to destroy the 44th Division began while mopping-up operations against the 163d were still in progress. On New Year's Eve a reinforced battalion of light infantry made a probing attack to the vicinity of the Haukila farm (see map 6). Skirting Lake Kuivasjärvi on the south, they encountered a Russian battalion east of the lake. They confirmed that the area was heavily defended. In fact, the largest concentration of the 44th Division—a reinforced regiment and most of the division's tanks and artillery—was strongly entrenched in a two-mile sector just east of the roadblock.

On 1 January a small reconnaissance unit reported that the enemy had occupied the Eskola area, about one and a half miles south of the Raate road on another road branching off from it and crossing the border to the southeast. To deny the Russians further use of that road, Siilasvuo immediately dispatched Capt. Ahti Paavola's light battalion to the Sanginlampi area, about three miles south of Eskola.

Now the winter road over the frozen lakes began to prove its worth. Paavola's troops easily skied along it for fifteen miles on New Year's Day, camping for the night near the Mäkelä farmhouse. Two larger strike groups, Task Forces Kari and Fagernäs, also skied along that ice road during the first two days of January. They deployed from Suomussalmi to positions as far as twenty miles to the southeast from which they would later launch coordinated flank attacks. Maj. Kaarle Kari's three battalions bivouacked in the Mäkelä area, while most of Lieutenant Colonel Fagernäs's two battalions camped near Heikkilä. One reinforced company went as far as Vänkä, just south of Raate.

All of those units enjoyed the comfort of Finnish Army tents, each of which was easily transported on one skifflike sled called an *akhio*, which was harnessed to three skiers, with a fourth behind it to steady the load. The units also used that simple carrier to haul mortars, heavy machine guns, and supplies and to evacuate the wounded. Each tent, heated by a wood-burning stove, kept twenty men comfortably warm on even the coldest nights. Lying on soft pine branches and sleeping in their uniforms, the Finns did not need blankets.

In marked contrast, the Russians huddled around open campfires or dug holes in the snow for shelter. At best, they had an improvised lean-to, a shallow hole covered with branches, or a branch hut fashioned at the roadside or in a ditch. The fortunate ones had a fire in a half barrel. Many literally froze to death in their sleep. Lack of proper footgear aggravated their misery; the summer leather boots which most wore contributed to many frostbite cases. Finnish estimates put Russian losses from the cold as high as their battle casualties. Once the Finns had begun major and sustained counterattacks, the enemy's problems of survival worsened: it became too dangerous to use open fires at night.

Numbering about a thousand men, Capt. Eino Lassila's battalion (I/JR27) began the first sustained effort to cut up the 44th Division during the night of 1 January. Using the winter road previously cleared around the southern end of Lake Kuivasjärvi and extending to the east, a rifle company moved ahead as a trail security party during the afternoon of 1 January. The remainder of the battalion followed about an hour later. By 1700 the entire battalion had reached the end of the horse trail (the winter road), where they ate a hot meal before proceeding to their objective some three miles to the north. Pulling machine guns and ammunition along on *akhios*, they traversed those last miles through dark woods in deep snow and bitter cold silently on skis.

About 2300 the advance guard reached a ridge about four hundred yards from the Raate road, where they could see the enemy grouped around numerous campfires. Captain Lassila positioned six heavy machine guns on each side of the assault force on the ridge. He ordered two rifle companies to advance abreast and very close to one another, while the third remained in reserve near the command post behind the ridge. Upon reaching the road, one company would push east, the other west, to seize about five hundred yards of the roadway. Then the attached engineer platoon would throw up roadblocks in both directions by felling trees and mining them.

A half hour after midnight the assault companies advanced, overran the sentries posted about sixty yards from the roadway, and reached the road with little opposition. By a fortunate accident they had emerged from the woods some five hundred yards east of their assigned objective, the Haukila farm. Instead of the strong infantry defenses they had expected, the Finns fell upon an artillery battalion, which they easily captured. When they struck the road all of the field guns were facing west; although the Russians managed to turn two pieces towards the south, their crews were shot down before they could fire a single round. The Soviet four-barreled antiaircraft machine guns were also ineffective because they were mounted so high on trucks that they fired over the Finns' heads. The Finnish assault companies completed their task in about two hours with only light casualties; they did not even need the reserve company.

Using the horse and sled method described above, the battalion supply troops worked all night long to extend the winter road from the end of the horse trail to the battle area. About 0700 the first priority shipment arrived via this route—two antitank guns. They saw action almost immediately when the Russians launched their first counterattack from the east. Within fifteen minutes they destroyed seven tanks on or near the road, making the roadblock even more effective. The Finns also beat off an infantry attack.

Later that morning hot meals were sent forward from the support area, and tents were erected behind the ridge. The troops then rotated so they could warm up and have hot tea inside those shelters. Except when under immediate attack, they were routinely relieved after two hours of exposure to the cold. In contrast, the Russians were both cold and hungry. Finnish patrols deliberately sought out field kitchens as targets and eventually destroyed or captured all fifty-five of them. Each day the roadblock held, the Russians grew weaker and more demoralized.*

During the afternoon of 2 January about two companies of Russian infantry waddled through deep snow to hit Lassila's roadblock from the west, but the Finnish reserve company caught them from the flank and forced them to withdraw. Then, as later, the 44th Division failed to coordinate its counterattacks and thus permitted the Finns to deal with them one at a time.

That same day Capt. Aarne Airimos's battalion (III/JR27) assaulted the road on Lassila's left flank and encountered the strong defenses near the Haukila farm. Although he secured positions close to the roadway, he could not sever it. That evening Colonel Siilasvuo ordered Capt. Sulo Häkkinen to position his light battalion (Sissi P1**) closer to Haukila, where it could support the 1st and 3d Battalions of the 27th Infantry Regiment. Häkkinen also sent reconnaissance patrols east of Lassila's roadblock.

Further to the southeast, on 2 January, Captain Paavola's light battalion advanced towards the Sanginlampi farmstead from Mäkelä. Because the Russians had deployed considerable forces there via the road past Eskola, Siilasvuo had to send Major Kari's units to assist Paavola. On 3 January Kari sent the 4th Replacement Battalion into the attack, and the next day it captured the Sanginlampi area in heavy fighting. Meanwhile, on 3 January one company of Sissi P1 cut the road north of Eskola, which enabled another of Kari's battalions (ER*** P15) to take Eskola from the south the next morning. Kari's third battalion (I/JR64) also reached Eskola that day. Thus, by 4 January Task Force Kari had secured an excellent attack position within two miles of the Kokkojärvi road fork.

---

*The Finnish term for such an entrapped enemy force is a *motti*, which is their word for a stack of firewood piled up to be chopped. *Motti* warfare became a common feature of the battles in the forested wilds north of Lake Ladoga. When the Finns lacked sufficient firepower to reduce strong *mottis*—some of which contained scores of tanks—they relied upon cold and hunger to destroy their enemies.

**Sissi literally means guerrilla, but it should not be equated to partisans; it was essentially light infantry employed in a manner similar to the U.S. Army Rangers, but Sissi units did not receive special training like the Rangers.
    P: Battalion

***ER: Indedpendent (Detached)

At the same time Task Force Fagernäs's battalions (II and III/JR64) had been improving communications from the base camps towards the Raate road, but not close enough to alert the enemy. The company at Vänkä constructed a winter road as far as Linnalampi, while the main units at Heikkilä opened a poor road part way to Honkajärvi. By 4 January both forces had relatively easy access to points within four miles of the Raate road.

On 4 January Colonel Siilasvuo issued orders for a general attack designed to destroy the 44th Division the next day. Two new task forces were assembled; Lieutenant Colonel Mäkiniemi's included all three battalions of his own regiment (JR27) plus the 1st Sissi Battalion (Sissi P1). Siilasvuo allocated six of his eight field guns to Mäkiniemi, because he had to attack the strongest known enemy concentration—in the Haukila area. Lieutenant Colonel Mandelin's Task Force, two battalions of JR65 and three separate units of company size or smaller, was to strike Haukila from the north in coordination with Mäkiniemi's blow from the south.

Just east of Mäkiniemi's sector, Task Force Kari—with three battalions and the remaining two field guns—was to destroy the strong units in the Kokkojärvi-Tyynelä region by flank attacks. With part of his force he was also to push east to link up with Task Force Fagernäs. Comprising two battalions of JR64, Task Force Fagernäs was supposed to cut the road about a mile from the border and at the Purasjoki River to prevent the 44th Division from receiving reinforcements from the east.

On the fifth, Soviet resistance was still so strong that none of those attacks succeeded completely. The Soviets checked three of Task Force Mäkiniemi's battalions as they closed on the Raate road east of the original roadblock. The fourth, Captain Lassila's battalion, which had been holding its stretch of the road since 2 January, lost ninety-six men that day as the Russians desperately attempted to break through to the east.

Attacking from the north, Task Force Mandelin also made little progress, although it did secure—too lightly, as it later developed—a minor road leading northeast to the border near Puras in order to block any Russian retreat in that direction. Task Force Kari's attacks in the Kokkojärvi and Tyynelä areas were likewise thrown back on the fifth; the Finns sustained heavy losses at Kokkojärvi.

Task Force Fagernäs achieved the day's best results, although it accomplished only half of its mission, its attacks in the Raate area and at Likoharju having been repelled. Near Mäntylä, however, one of its platoons did ambush and destroy several truckloads of reinforcements that were part of the 3d NKVD* Regiment, which had been sent to assist the 44th Division

---

*NKVD: People's Commissariat of Internal Affairs, which included both secret police and border guard formations.

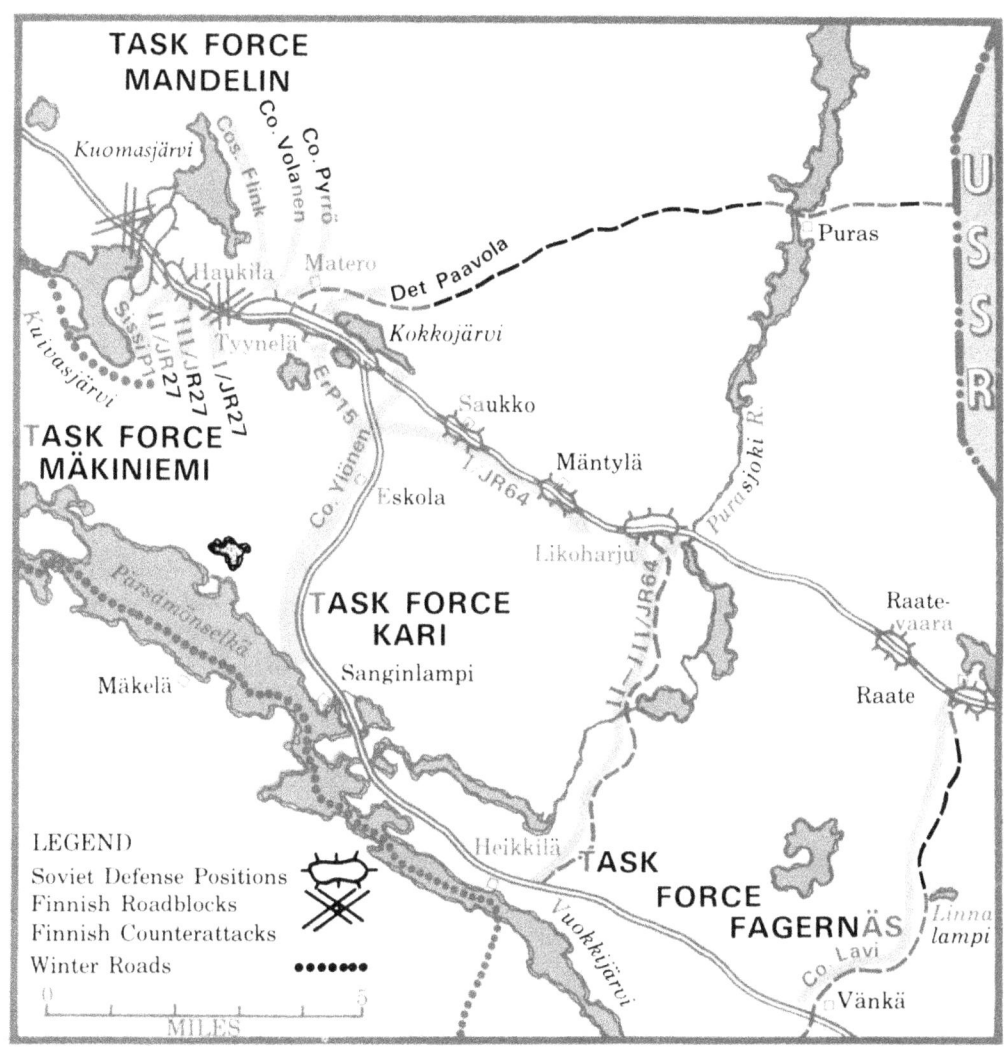

Map 6. Destruction of the 44th Division.

at the beginning of January. In a renewed assault that night, Fagernäs finally took a stretch of the Raate road just north of Likoharju and held it against a strong counterattack from the east. Around 2200, his engineers blew up the Purasjoki River bridge, thus preventing further enemy truck traffic beyond that point (the river banks were too steep for motor vehicles).

The decisive battles occurred on 6 January. Task Force Mäkiniemi overcame stubborn resistance to widen its hold on the Raate road east of the original roadblock. By evening all four of its battalions had reached the road, and the 3d Battalion had established a roadblock west of the one the 1st Battalion was still defending against repeated attacks. About 0200 the next day the Finns resumed the offensive, and after an hour's battle the enemy troops facing the 2d and 3d Battalions (JR27) abandoned their heavy equipment on the road and fled towards Haukila hill.

On the opposite side of the road, Task Force Mandelin spent most of 6 January hunting down enemy stragglers who were retreating through the woods to the northeast. Trudging through the snow on foot, the demoralized Russians were easy prey for the Finnish skiers.

About 0300 on 6 January, a reinforced company of Task Force Kari cut the Raate road about a mile east of Kokkojärvi and established another roadblock, which it held against two strong counterattacks. Desperately trying to fight its way out to the east, the 44th Division was being cut into smaller and smaller fragments. Battalion ERP15 seized a segment of the road east of Tyynelä about 1100, after a three-hour battle. The main forces of the battalion then turned west towards Tyynelä. By afternoon the Russians were abandoning this sector and fleeing along the Puras road, where only two Finnish companies were screening a broad sector. Colonel Siilasvuo therefore sent Captain Paavola's detachment to block that escape route at Matero, which Paavola reached that evening.

The freshest Russian troops, including the NKVD unit, counterattacked Task Force Fagernäs in such strength during the morning of 6 January that it had to withdraw a short distance into the woods to escape the fire of five Russian tanks. After their reserve company arrived, the Finns resumed the offensive near the Purasjoki bridge, where they established defensive positions west of the river. Nevertheless, Russian counterattacks continued near Likoharju late into the evening.

To relieve the pressure on Fagernäs, Siilasvuo ordered Kari to send a battalion (I/JR64) against the enemy who were operating between those two task forces. That understrength battalion advanced along a forest path from Eskola to Saukko. Overcoming stiff resistance there, it pushed on by evening to Mäntylä, which it took after several hours of fighting. By then so many Russian stragglers had bypassed the roadblock east of Kokkojärvi through the woods that they threatened the battalion's rear. Therefore, late in the evening the battalion commander turned his front from east to west and destroyed those harassing groups. The company near Raate also resumed its attacks on 6 January to prevent Russian movement on the road near the border.

Late in the evening of the sixth, Commander Vinogradov belatedly authorized the retreat that had been underway in many sectors for hours. He advised his subordinate commanders that the situation was desperate and that those who could escape should.

Although only mopping-up was necessary in most sectors on 7 January, the Russians were still trying to fight their way through to the east near Likoharju. About 0400, with the help of tanks, they threw a Finnish company back from the Purasjoki River. However, a Finnish counterattack at 1030 that morning dispersed the Russians in disorder. The Finns then continued westward to capture Likoharju, where they took many prisoners and five tanks.

The final attempt to rescue the 44th Division came during the early morning darkness when infantry, supported by artillery positioned behind the border, assaulted the company at Raate. After repelling that attack, the Finns sent a reconnaissance patrol two miles inside Soviet territory, where it encountered only support elements.

There was also minor fighting near Lake Kokkojärvi and Tyynelä early on 7 January, but the Russians knew they were doomed. At daylight, troops of Task Force Mäkiniemi crossed the Raate road near Haukila and pushed north until they linked up with Task Force Mandelin.

The Russians in bunkers along the shore of Lake Kuivasjärvi resisted stubbornly, but the Finns cleared that area during the day and opened the road to Suomussalmi. The last organized resistance came from bunkers near Lake Kuomasjärvi. A Finnish platoon dispatched late in the evening returned from those positions at 0400 on the eighth with seventy prisoners.

Mopping-up continued for several days, as the Finns hunted down half-frozen stragglers in the woods along the entire length of the Raate road and to the north. By the standards of that small war, the booty was enormous: the Finns captured 43 tanks, 70 field guns, 278 trucks, cars, and tractors, some 300 machine guns, 6,000 rifles, 1,170 live horses, and modern communication equipment which was especially prized. The enemy dead could not even be counted because of the snow drifts that covered the fallen and the wounded who had frozen to death. A conservative Finnish estimate put the combined Russian losses (the 163d and 44th Divisions, plus the 3d NKVD Regiment) at 22,500 men. Counting killed, wounded, and missing, Finnish losses were approximately 2,700 (only about 12 percent of these casualties were frostbite cases).

Debris of the 44th Division along the Raate road

Additional features of winter combat demonstrated in this classic battle include:

- The great utility of skis: The relative immobility of troops not trained to use skis affected intelligence as well as deployment. Finnish ski patrols kept their road-bound enemy under continuous surveillance, whereas the Russians remained ignorant of the Finnish strength and dispositions.

- The effectiveness of improvised roads: In terrain where trucks fitted with snowplows could not get through, the simple method of compacting snow with a series of horse-drawn sleds was quite effective.

- The advantages of specialized training and equipment: Sleeping on pine boughs in heated tents kept the Finns comfortable while their opponents were literally freezing to death a few hundred yards away.

- Unusual targeting: The Finns accelerated their enemy's debilitation by firing on his campfires and destroying his field kitchens.

The Russians had reason to regret the folly of launching their invasion without thorough preparations to cope with the environment, but they were not the last to make that costly mistake.

Pertinent Aspects of Nazi-Soviet Warfare During the Winter of 1941—42

During the fifteen-month interval between the Winter War and Hitler's invasion of Russia, the Red Army profited from its experience in Finland. In addition to making general organizational and tactical changes, the Soviets paid more attention to winter clothing, equipment, and training—including that of ski troops—in marked contrast to their future opponents.

Many of the combat problems the German Army encountered in European Russia during the winter of 1941—42 resemble a greatly amplified playback of the Arkhangelsk campaign of 1918—19. The Germans paid an exorbitant price for ignoring the lessons of those, and other, earlier winter campaigns. General Dr. Waldemar Erfurth noted that before 1941 the German General Staff had never been interested in the history of wars in northern and eastern Europe. No accounts of the wars of Russia against the Swedes, Finns, and Poles had been published in German. "The older generation which had been brought up in the tradition of von Moltke . . . considered it sufficient to study the countries immediately surrounding Germany. . . . the northern regions of Europe remained practically unknown to the German soldier."[1]

The devastating results of the decision to expose German troops to combat in the latitude of Moscow—the same as that of Hudson Bay in Canada—without appropriate clothing and provisions were so widespread that it is impossible to single out one particular battle as the best example. Accordingly, the observations that follow are generalizations applicable to a very wide front.

Weather

In 1941 winter weather arrived in Russia earlier* than usual.[2] Initially, that was not entirely detrimental to German operations, because it cut short the autumn *rasputitsa*, the period of heavy rains which twice a year turns the unpaved roads of central and northern Russia into an impassable

---

*In normal years, snows begin in central European Russia about mid-November and severe cold sets in during the latter half of December.

Map 7. The Soviet Winter Offensive, 1941–42.

morass of mud. The temperature dropped sharply at the beginning of November, causing the roads to freeze, thus allowing the movement of trucks and tanks.[3]

Although there is general agreement concerning weather conditions on the Russian front through October 1941, there are many conflicting versions of the severity of temperatures during the weeks and months that followed. For example, Field Marshal von Bock, commander of Army Group Center, recorded in his war diary on 5 November 1941 that the mercury dipped to -29°C (-20°F),[4] and Albert Seaton reported that around 24 November it was a steady -30°C (22°F).[5] In contrast, Marshal Zhukov, then responsible for defending the approaches to Moscow, stated that during the November general offensive the temperature on the Moscow front remained stable at -7° to -10°C (+19° to +14°F).[6] In a work specifically refuting German accounts, another Soviet spokesman cites these Meteorological Service records of the minimum temperatures for the Moscow area in late 1941: October, -8.2°C (about +17°F); November, -17.3°C (+1°F); December, -28.8°C (-20°F).[7] There were also many reports of temperatures as low as -40° during that exceptionally cold winter,[8] and at least one report of -53°C (-63°F).[9]

In terms of casualties, the precise temperatures are virtually meaningless, because a poorly clothed soldier exposed to the elements is susceptible to frostbite even at temperatures warmer than -18°C (0°F). As previously noted, the Allies suffered more frostbite casualties during the fighting around Bolshie Ozerki from late March through early April 1919—when the lowest temperature was only -20°C (-4°F) and daytime thawing caused wet boots—than they experienced during the coldest periods of that winter.

There had been some snowfall as early as October 1941,[10] and heavy, cumulative snows began about 7 December. Strong winds and blizzards followed, creating massive drifts.[11] The exceptional cold caused the snow to remain unusually powdery and deep long after it had fallen.[12] Marshal Emerenko estimated the winter's lasting snow cover in the region between Moscow and Leningrad at .7 to 1.5 meters (28—59 inches).[13] This snow cover greatly restricted German mobility,[14] but it also hampered the Red Army. One German source frankly states that the fate of the overextended Army Group Center would have been even worse had there been less snow, concluding that "complete collapse [of the German units] was prevented . . . especially by the deep snow, which constituted a major obstacle [to the Soviet counteroffensive]."[15] Discussing the plight of about seven divisions that were cut off in January 1942, a German commander observed that "the deep snows protected the encircled German troops around Demyansk from annihilation. Even the Russian infantry was unable to launch an attack through those snows."[16]

Weather-Related Casualties

Hitler's overconfidence immeasurably compounded the inevitable hardships of a winter campaign in Russia. Expecting victory by autumn, he had intended to withdraw two-thirds of his divisions from Russia and to leave the remainder as an occupation army. Winter clothing, procured on the basis of the occupation force, arrived very late because of the breakdown in transportation.[17] On 30 November von Bock informed Field Marshal von Brauchitsch, the Chief of Staff of the German Army, that his men still had not received winter coats, although the temperature was -45°C (-49°F).[18] Nearly three weeks later the angry General Heinz Guderian, commander of the Second Panzer Army, confronted Hitler with the stark facts that none of the winter clothing had yet arrived in the forward areas and that he had lost twice as many men from frost as from enemy action. That conversation led to the Nazi Party's Christmas drive among German civilians to collect winter clothes and skis,[19] few of which reached the front before February 1942. The freezing German troops were reduced to removing clothes from enemy corpses,[20] improvising straw boots, and taking other emergency measures.[21]

It is no wonder that thousands of Germans froze to death that winter.[22] By the turn of the year they had suffered about 100,000 cases of frostbite, more than 14,000 of which required amputations.[23] By the end of that terrible winter the number of frostbite victims exceeded a quarter of a million, and more than 90 percent were second- and third-degree cases.[24] To these must be added thousands of cases of pneumonia, influenza, and trench-foot.[25]

The impact of those non-battle casualties was tremendous. Although the Red Army had lost millions in dead, wounded, and captured by December 1941, Russia was able to muster replacements from its vast manpower resources. In contrast, by 26 November German losses of about 375,000 dead, missing, and permanently disabled were virtually irreplaceable. By April 1942 the German deficiency on the Russian front had reached 625,000 men.[26] In the words of a German officer who survived that grueling winter, those casualties meant that "the actual loss of the war in the East merely had been postponed."[27]

The Red Army was far better prepared for winter warfare than were its opponents. For example, Siberian troops who attacked the shivering Germans of the 35th Infantry Division near Moscow on 5 December 1941 wore padded jackets and trousers, fur caps, and felt boots.[28] Nevertheless, the unseasonable cold of early November caught many Russian units by surprise. On 9 November Marshal Kirill Meretskov, then commanding both the Fourth and Seventh Armies, personally checked the condition of the troops who had lost the town of Tikhvin the previous day. He found the troops still in summer uniforms.[29] A week later a German attack on a hill northeast of Rzhev succeeded because the Soviet sentries, who had not yet received winter clothes, were too cold to be alert.[30] However, winter uniforms were available at Russian supply points, and distribution was soon accomplished.[31]

Camouflaged Soviet troops in attack, winter 1941—42

Nevertheless, Soviet troops also suffered weather-related casualties. The diary of a Red Army field surgeon contains the 27 January 1942 notation that "the first frostbite cases have made their appearance. We amputated two feet and will probably amputate many more."[32] The main cause of such losses was the Soviet counteroffensive that began early in December and continued throughout the coldest months of the winter. General Ironside's observations in 1919 about the superiority of the defense over the offense in such weather remained valid. A German officer who witnessed persistent Soviet attacks near Shuvaevo in mid-January 1942, when the temperature reached -40°, reported that "the Russians suffered even more [than the Germans] from the cold despite their winter clothing, since they were out in the open."[33]

Logistics and Mobility

The ubiquitous, shaggy, hardy Russian ponies once more proved indispensable for transport in bad weather. Many of the larger horses that the Germans had brought from western Europe died from the cold, but the native breed could survive in the open at almost any temperature if merely sheltered from the wind.[34] The Germans called those small, patient animals *panje* horses, a term they also applied to the native carts and sleighs.[35] German accounts were full of praise for those seemingly anachronistic vehicles and horses. General Rendulic wrote:

The light native carts (sleighs), and the small, strong, and undemanding native horses are absolutely indispensable for the trains of infantry units. They are equally indispensable for the supply of motorized troops during the muddy season and in the winter, whenever military operations grind to a halt. Before long, even the German motorized and armored divisions had such trains of horse-drawn vehicles at their disposal. I cannot imagine how the German Army could have fought and lived through four years of war against Russia if it had not made use of these carts, sleighs, and horses.[36]

German supply column returning from the front, January 1942

In the opinion of another German officer, *panje* sleighs were not only the best means of transport in winter, but in the open fields and on the miserable secondary roads they were the *only* vehicles that afforded complete oversnow mobility.[37] By early 1942 some panzer divisions employed as many as two thousand *panje* horses, while hardly any of their motor vehicles remained serviceable. Those panzer units were given the ironic nickname *panje* divisions. Even the Luftwaffe had to resort to *panje* transport in Russia.[38]

Naturally, the Russians relied upon the same horse-drawn transport, but they also employed cavalry in combat. A German source even reported a quixotic mounted cavalry attack against a German tank company in January 1942.[39] For security and reconnaissance missions, the Soviets used cavalry units extensively. At times these troops fought dismounted. They also cooperated with armor in major offensive operations.[40]

Russian tanks, especially the T34, KV1, and KV2, were effective even in deep snow because of their wide tracks and good ground clearance. These features gave them a marked advantage over the tanks that the Germans employed during the first winter, tanks which became stuck because of their narrow tracks and limited ground clearance. The Soviets frequently used T34s to break paths through the snow for the infantry.[41]

Another advantage the Russians enjoyed was the number of ski troops. Profiting from the lessons of the Winter War against the Finns, both Soviet military and civilian authorities emphasized skiing during the peacetime winter of 1940—41. Special ski units, trained in Siberia and committed on the Finnish front during the new war, proved almost as skillful as the Finns.[42]

The Soviets employed ski troops in units up to brigade size.[43] In January 1942 a force of three ski battalions was operating behind the German Fourth Army.[44] On the night of 23 November 1941 about three hundred skiers, including female Komsomol students and Party workers, executed a daring raid on 12th Corps headquarters, killing nineteen Germans and wounding twenty-nine. Although their casualties were heavy, 80 percent of the skiers made their way back through the woods.[45]

Other ski units were not always that lucky. A ski brigade of the 39th Guards Army that made a dawn attack on the rear of the 114th Panzer Grenadier Regiment in late March 1942 was virtually annihilated. It failed to surprise the Germans partly because they clearly heard its approach over the snow, for sound travels a great distance in cold weather.[46] (Powdery snow tends to reduce the sound of movement, but that is not true of the heavy crusted snow common by early spring.)

Russian ski units were more successful in combination with other arms. When the Third Panzer Army was retreating west of Moscow in December 1941, a Russian force of ski troops, cavalry, and sleigh-mounted infantry cut off the 6th Panzer Division, which was the rear guard of the LVI Panzer Corps.[47]

Although the mobility of well-trained ski units was a significant asset, not all of the Russian ski troops employed in that first wartime winter were sufficiently experienced to exploit that advantage. General Meretskov noted that he often saw men of the hastily formed Second and Fifty-ninth Shock Armies proceeding on foot, dragging their skis behind them.[48]

The Germans found it even more difficult to muster effective ski troops, which they did not employ in units larger than battalions.[49] Within Army Group Center, accounts of one regiment reveal that it had only ten sets of ski equipment per company in January 1942.[50] Another regiment could equip only one platoon per unit, barely enough for patrol, messenger, and similar duties.[51] When a corps was finally able to organize one ski battalion in March 1942, the men had to be selected on the basis of their skiing ability. Because many were from support units—with no combat experience—their effectiveness was limited.[52]

Weather-Related Failures of Arms and Machines

It could only have been in total ignorance of the Arkhangelsk campaign more than twenty-two years earlier that the German Army in 1941 could be "surprised" (as General Rendulic expressed it) that because of the extreme cold the mechanisms of rifles and machine guns, and even the breech blocks of artillery, became absolutely rigid.[53] The recoil liquid in artillery pieces also froze stiff,[54] and tempered steel parts cracked.[55] Strikers and striker springs broke like glass.[56]

One can only conjecture the number of tactical defeats such surprises caused. Even General Halder took notice of an encounter near Tikhvin when the temperature was -35°C (-31°F) and only one of the five German tanks could fire.[57] Sentries in the German 196th Infantry Regiment discovered at the inopportune moment of a Soviet night attack in January 1942 that their machine guns were too frozen to function.[58]

Soviet weapons were designed for winter, and they used appropriate lubricants. The Germans preferred the Soviet submachine gun to the model originally issued to them.[59] During the first winter the Germans had to improvise by lighting fires under their artillery, and by either wiping off all the lubricants from weapons or experimenting with substitutes. Kerosene worked, but it was not durable and thus had to be renewed frequently.[60] Sunflower oil proved quite effective, but it was available only in southern Russia.[61] (By the second winter of the war the Germans had suitable lubricants on hand.[62])

Deep snow greatly reduced the effectiveness of mortar shells, and even of artillery smaller than 150-mm caliber. The best antitank weapon was the gun of a heavy tank, for regular antitank artillery could not be used in deep snow.[63] Mines proved unreliable under heavy snow or ice, especially when there was some thawing, because their pressure fuses would not function when cushioned by deep snow or covered with an ice crust.[64]

As noted, the oversnow capabilities of Soviet tanks were superior to those of the German models employed in 1941. The Germans also encountered constant problems with most of their motor vehicles. At first they tried to start frozen machines by towing, which badly damaged motors and ripped differentials to pieces. It proved necessary to apply heat for up to two hours before moving.[65] During alerts motors were frequently kept running for hours.[66] (Only the *panje* horse started without a warming up period!)

German vehicles abandoned during the retreat from Moscow, December 1941

Weather's Impact on Local Operations and Tactics

Because shelter was essential to survival, villages became the focal points of local battles during the winter of 1941—42, just as they had been in 1918—19.[67] During the Soviet counteroffensive General Rendulic, commander of the 52d Infantry Division, initially tried to conduct an orthodox defense which included holding open terrain. That, however, led to so many frostbite casualties that he had to restrict his lines to populated points and their immediate environs. When the Russians penetrated the gaps between the German-held villages and fanned out laterally to threaten the roads leading to the rear of those villages, the Germans were forced to retreat again. Where the Soviet forces had sufficient ammunition and passable roads, they also attacked the villages.[68] Whenever they failed to capture them during the day, they usually withdrew to the nearest friendly village for the night.[69]

Whenever the Germans were able to take the initiative, they faced the same problem, though aggravated because of their inferior clothing. On 28 December 1941 the 4th Armored Infantry Regiment of the 6th Panzer Division successfully counterattacked Russian units that had broken through the German positions on the Lama River. By evening they closed the gap in their line by making contact with the 23d Infantry Division, and they sheltered that night in nearby villages and farmhouses. The plan for the next day was to surround the enemy and regain the Lama River positions. Again the 4th Infantry, in an attack coordinated with the division's motorcycle battalion, attained its objectives: by noon the Soviet breakthrough force was encircled. The nearby villages had been destroyed, however, and the former positions were buried deep in show. Without shelter, and faced with freezing to death in the nighttime temperature of -30° to -40°, the Germans had to abandon the encirclement and withdraw to a distant village. The Russians then broke through again and eventually forced the entire German front in that area to withdraw. Battlefield success had turned to failure because the Germans were not equipped for the weather and could not find local shelter.[70]

Occasionally even a destroyed village offered protection from the cold. The Russians generally tried to surround a German-held village before the garrison could escape and set it on fire. When they failed and the village burned, they usually arrived before the fires had died down, and they could begin at once to dig shelters in the ground thawed by the heat.[71]

Sometimes there was an alternative to shelter in villages, even when the ground was too hard for digging. Conducting defensive operations in open country around the turn of the year, the 6th Panzer Division was sustaining about 800 frostbite casualties a day. It had some five tons of explosives on hand, however, and on 3 January 1942 its engineers blasted enough craters to accommodate all of the combat elements. Covered with lumber and heated with open fires, each crater sheltered three to five men. New frostbite cases immediately fell from eight hundred to four a day. With minefields, antitank obstacles, and paths trampled between and behind the craters, the position held out for ten days and was only abandoned when outflanked.[72] Eventually, in order to free them from dependence on the engineers, the Germans trained both combat and service units to use 100-gram cartridges for blasting shelters.[73]

The Germans soon learned how to prevent wood smoke from revealing their field positions. In contrast to fresh firewood, charcoal burns with little smoke and its manufacture was improvised widely.[74]

Deep snow hampered movement on foot. In one instance a unit of the 52d Infantry Division required nine hours to advance two and one-half miles—unopposed—through five feet of snow. Consequently, trampling lateral and rearward paths assumed tactical significance. For example, the German commander of Company G, 464th Infantry, realized on 15 January 1942 that his positions would soon become untenable. He therefore detailed a few men with minor wounds to trample a path from the village held by the company towards a nearby forest. During the ensuing Soviet offensive, that path prevented his unit from being trapped by the enemy.[75]

Distinctive lessons which may be drawn from this chapter include:

- Sound travels farther in very cold weather. On the Russian front in World War II the noise of troops advancing over heavy, crusted snow deprived them of the advantage of surprise.
- Horses provided the most reliable transport on the Russian front in winter. The small but acclimatized native horses proved superior to larger breeds accustomed to the milder climate of Western Europe.
- Mines often failed in winter. This was true when the snow was sufficiently deep to cushion the fuse and when alternating melting and freezing created an ice bridge over the detonator.
- Charcoal was better than wood for heating because it created less smoke to reveal troop positions.
- Soviet wide-tracked tanks had better over-snow mobility than the early German models because of their lighter ground pressure.
- Explosives were useful for constructing foxholes and larger shelters in frozen ground.
- Finally, perhaps the most important lesson is simply the folly of ignoring the pertinent lessons. A former Luftwaffe officer, Lt. Gen. H. J. Rieckhoff, concluded a discussion of the problems encountered by the ground components of the German Air Force in winter with the observation that the highest German commanders were slow to profit from Russian examples because of their feeling of superiority, and some refused to learn until they went down in defeat.[76] There may be a message for others in that conceit.

German troops in retreat, December 1941

Conclusion

These cases illustrate common lessons, even though they span almost a quarter of a century, cover a broad geographic area, and concern arms ranging from bayonets to modern tanks. Foremost among these lessons is that troops fighting in severe winter weather must have appropriate clothing, weapons, and transport for that harsh environment. Acclimatization and pertinent training are also essential.

Two of the three campaigns clearly demonstrated the superiority of the defense over the offense in such weather conditions. The exception, the destruction of the 44th Division, does not invalidate that generalization: the attacking Finns enjoyed concealment and warm shelter in the woods, whereas the Russians were defending a hopeless position, an exposed roadway without sheltering villages. Most of the weather-related casualties of 1941–42 need not have occurred had the commanders fully appreciated the experiences of 1918–19. Most of those lessons will probably be valid as long as Russian winters remain frigid. Surely "General Winter" will always be a formidable foe to an unwary army fighting in Russia.

Notes

Introduction

[1] Eugene Tarlé, *Napoleon's Invasion of Russia—1812* (London: George Allen and Unwin Ltd., 1942), p. 40; *Sovetskaya Voennaya Entsiklopediya* [Soviet military encyclopedia], 6 (Moscow: Voennoe Izdatel'stvo, 1978):153 (hereafter cited as *SovVoenEnts*).

[2] Eugene Tarlé, *Bonaparte* (New York: Knight Publications, 1937), p. 271.

[3] Theodore Dodge, *Napoleon* (Boston: Houghton Mifflin and Co., 1907), 3:479, 507.

[4] *SovVoenEnts*, 1(1976):567. Count Philippe DeSégur, *Napoleon's Russian Campaign,* trans. J. David Townsend (Boston: Houghton Mifflin and Co., 1958), gives French strength at Borodino as only 120,000.

[5] Andrei Lobanov-Rostovsky, *Russia and Europe 1789—1825* (Durham: Duke University Press, 1947), p. 223. DeSégur, p. 98, puts Napoleon's losses at 40,000. Soviet estimates of French losses range from 50,000 to 58,578. See *SovVoenEnts*, 1:569; L. G. Beskrovnyi, *Otechestvennaya Voina 1812 Goda* [The fatherland war of 1812] (Moscow: SOTSEKGIZ, 1962), p. 397.

[6] Tarlé, *Bonaparte*, p. 296.

[7] DeSégur, p. 167; Dodge, p. 646.

[8] Franz Halder, *The Halder Diaries: The Private War Journals of Col. Gen. Franz Halder* (Boulder, Colo.: Westview Press, 1977), 2:187 (7:1321 of original).

[9] Ibid., p. 183 (p. 1317).

[10] Col. Frances King discusses many of these constant factors in their modern context in "Cold Weather Warfare: What Would Happen?" *Military Review* 57 (November 1977):86—95.

Chapter 1

Chapter 1 contains many citations from National Archives Record Group 120, Records of the American Expeditionary Forces (World War I), 1917—1923, which includes a collection known as the Historical File of the AEF, North Russia (hereafter cited as Archives). The following abbreviations pertain to these records:

"Extracts"—"Extracts from Correspondence Files of Allied G.H.Q. Archangel" (file 23-11.5).

"Records"—"Records of Events, 'M' Co., 339th Infantry Regiment" (file 23-33.2, item 17-F).

"Operation Report"—"Operation Report, 'H' Co., 339th Infantry Regiment, Apr 7, 1919" (file 23-33.2, item 17-J).

"Summary"—"Summary of principal military events . . . Aug 4th, 1918 to and including March 24, 1919," forwarded to War Department by Colonel Ruggles, military attaché (file 23-33.6).

"Turner Report"—"Report of Major H. C. Turner, O. C. Bolshieozerka Det., dated April 9th, 1919, covering March 31st to April 1st" (file 23-33.2, item 17-E).

"War Diary"—"War Diary, G.H.Q., Notes-Shenkursk Evacuation" (file 23-33.2, item 15-A).

[1]Leonid A. Strakhovsky, *Intervention at Archangel* (New York: Howard Fertig, 1971), pp. 167—77, 194, 280—84; Richard H. Ullman, *Anglo-Soviet Relations, 1917—21: Intervention and the War* (Princeton: Princeton University Press, 1961), 1:109, 252, 2:198—99.

[2]Ullman, 1:243.

[3]Strakhovsky, pp. 44—45, 283—84; Ullman, 1:252; A. A. Samoilo and M. I. Sboichakov, *Pouchitel'nyi Urok* (Moscow, 1962), p. 116; Archives, "Report of Expedition to the Murman Coast," compiled by Lt. Col. E. Lewis, 339th Infantry (file 23-33.2), strength return for 3 June 1919; Leonid Strakhovsky, "The Canadian Artillery Brigade in North Russia," *The Canadian Historical Review*, June 1958, p. 127.

[4]Samoilo and Sboichakov, pp. 8, 177; *Direktivy Komandovaniya Frontov Krasnoi Armii (1917—1922)* [Directives of the command of the Red Army fronts (1917—1922)], ed. V. V. Dushen'kin et al., 4 vols. (Moscow: Voennoe Izdatel'stvo, 1971—78), extrapolated from 4:33, 51 (hereafter cited as *Direktivy*).

[5]V. V. Tarasov, *Bor'ba s Interventami na Severe Rossii* [Combat with the interventionists in the north of Russia] (Moscow: GOSPOLITIZDAT, 1958), p. 157. Brig. Gen. Wilds P. Richardson, "Expedition in North Russia," Thomas Files, Historical Division Files, U.S. Army War College, Carlisle Barracks, Pa. (microfilm no. 51315), p. 33.

[6]E. M. Halliday, *The Ignorant Armies* (New York: Award Books, 1964), pp. 100, 101, 113—17, 123.

[7]William Edmund Ironside, *Archangel 1918—1919* (London: Constable and Co. Ltd., 1953), pp. 54, 55, 65.

[8]Lt. Col. Joel R. Moore, "The North Russian Expedition," *Infantry Journal*, July 1926, p. 19.

[9]Halliday, pp. 245—47.

[10]"Summary," 17 March entry; A. A. Veresov, ed., *Nezabyvaemye Imena* [Unforgettable names] (Arkhangelsk: Severo-Zapadnoe Knizhnoe Izdat., 1967), pp. 187—90.

[11]Ironside, p. 121.

[12]"Summary," 18 March entry.

[13]*Direktivy*, 2:21.

[14]Ibid., p. 22.

[15]Halliday, pp. 247—48; Archives, Captain Ballensinger's "Report of engagement," 24 March 1919 (file 23-33.2, item 17-H).

[16]"Summary," 23 March entry; Archives, Lieutenant Pellegrom's "Situation Report," 26 March 1919 (file 23-33.2, item 17-G); Capt. Joel R. Moore et al., eds., *The History of the American Expedition Fighting the Bolsheviki* (Detroit: Polar Bear Pub. Co., 1920), pp. 189—90.

[17]Ironside, pp. 121—22.

[18]Lieutenant Colonel Moore, *Infantry Journal*, p. 19; "Turner Report," p. 5.

[19]Compiled from Archives, "Weekly Order of Battle, Allied Forces, Archangel District, Northern Russia," dated 18 April 1919 (file 23-10.6).

[20]Lieutenant Colonel Moore, *Infantry Journal*, p. 19.

[21]Tarasov, p. 197.

[22]*Direktivy*, 2:22; "Turner Report," p. 4.

[23]*Direktivy*, 2:22; A. S. Bubnov et al., *Grazhdanskaya Voina 1918—1921* [Civil war 1918—1921] (Moscow: Izd. "Voennyi Vestnik," 1928), 1:227.

[24]Bubnov, 1:227; Captain Moore, p. 190.

[25]"Turner Report," pp. 1—3; "Records," 31 March entry.

[26]Captain Moore, pp. 170, 191.

[27]"Turner Report," p. 4.

[28]Archives, Lieutenant Colonel Morrison's Operations Order No. 1, 1 April 1919 (file 23-33.2); Lieutenant Colonel Morrison's "Report . . . on the Opertions West of Bolshieozerki on the 2d April, 1919" (file 23-33.2, item 17-D).

[29]"Operation Report," pp. 1—3.

[30]Captain Moore, pp. 171, 301.

[31]"Operation Report," p. 5; Lieutenant Colonel Morrison, "Report . . . . "

[32]Captain Moore, p. 192; "Records," pp. 3—4.

[33]Halliday, p. 251.

[34]Bubnov, 1:227.

[35] Ironside, p. 123.
[36] Bubnov, 1:227.
[37] Captain Moore, p. 192; Halliday, p. 151.
[38] Bubnov, 1:227.
[39] Halliday, pp. 87—88.
[40] "War Diary," p. 5.
[41] Halliday, p. 134.
[42] Ironside, pp. 99—100.
[43] A. Samoilo, *Dve Zhizny* [Two lives] (Moscow: Voennoe Izdatel'stvo, 1958), p. 240.
[44] *Sovetskaya Istoricheskaya Entsiklopediya* [Soviet historical encyclopedia], vol. 16 (Moscow, 1976), col. 253.
[45] "War Diary," p. 3; *Direktivy*, 1:507.
[46] Samoilo, p. 239.
[47] Archives, Lieutenant Steele's report, "Attack on Shegovari," 2 May 1919 (file 23-33.2, item 15-B).
[48] Bubnov, 1:222.
[49] Ibid., p. 224.
[50] Samoilo and Sboichakov, p. 87.
[51] One Soviet source (Bubnov, p. 225) shows Filippovsky with six heavy and eight light guns.
[52] *Direktivy*, 1:507, 778; Samoilo, p. 239.
[53] *Direktivy*, 1:508.
[54] Halliday, pp. 170—71; "Extracts," pp. 22—23; Archives, "Report of Expedition to the Murman Coast," p. 36. Nizhnyaya Gora is designated *Nizhni* Gora in many English-language sources, but the latter form is grammatically unlikely. Vysokaya Gora appears as *Visorka* Gora in many English works.
[55] Bubnov, 1:224.
[56] Halliday, pp. 170—71.
[57] Ibid., p. 170; Samoilo, p. 239.
[58] Ironside, p. 100; Halliday, p. 171.
[59] Halliday, pp. 171—75.
[60] "War Diary," p. 1.
[61] "Extracts," pp. 22—23.
[62] Halliday, p. 177.
[63] Samoilo and Sboichakov, p. 89.
[64] Ibid., pp. 177—79.
[65] Ibid., p. 185.
[66] Ironside, p. 102.
[67] Samoilo, p. 240—his dating is in error here.
[68] Ironside, p. 102; Halliday, pp. 185 ff.
[69] Halliday, pp. 187, 190—92; Samoilo, p. 240; Tarasov, p. 195.
[70] Halliday, pp. 148, 190; Ironside, p. 63.
[71] Samoilo, p. 240.
[72] Bubnov, 1:226.
[73] Samoilo and Sboichakov, p. 93.
[74] Captain Moore, p. 201; Capt. Donald A. Stroh, "A Critical Analysis of the North Russian Expedition . . . ," Individual Research Study No. 12, Command and General Staff School, Fort Leavenworth, Kans., 1933, pp. 26—27.
[75] Lt. W. K. M. Leader, "With the Murmansk Expeditionary Force," *Journal of the Royal United Service Institution*, February—November 1921, p. 666.
[76] *Direktivy*, 1:516—18.
[77] Maj. Frederic Evans, "Campaigning in Arctic Russia," *Journal of the Royal United Service Institution*, May 1941, p. 295.
[78] Archives, Captain Price's report, "Allied Offensive on Vologda Force Front," (inclosure to Colonel Ruggles's letter of 14 January 1919), (file 23-27.8), p. 7; Archives, Major Nichols's letter of 16 May 1919, "Operations of Railway Detachment December 30th and 31st, 1918" (file 23-33.2); Halliday, pp. 135—36, 142.

[79]Archives, Lt. John J. Baker's "Report of Engagement," 5 March 1919 (file 23-33.2, item 14-G), p. 3.
[80]Captain Moore, p. 68.
[81]Ibid., p. 190; Halliday, pp. 207—8, 251.
[82]This section was not intended to be an operational history of the North Russian campaign, but simply an examination of some of the most serious problems created by the environment. The less dramatic operations of the Allied force based on the ice-free port of Murmansk are briefly described by Lt. W. Leader in "With the Murmansk Expeditionary Force," pp. 662—91.

Chapter 2

[1]This section was adapted almost entirely from Chapter IV of the author's book, *The White Death: The Epic of the Soviet-Finnish Winter War* (East Lansing: Michigan State University Press, 1971), pp. 97—125. Because most of the sources cited therein are in the Finnish language they are not listed here. The additions to the above consist of a few technical details obtained in more recent correspondence between the author and Colonel Eino Lassila, USA (Ret.), who—as a captain in the Finnish Army—participated in the battles on the Raate Road.

Chapter 3

This section uses numerous unpublished or limited-distribution monographs from the Foreign Military Studies series. Written in the years immediately following World War II by former German officers who had fought on the Russian front, the monographs were produced under the auspices of the Office of the Chief Historian, Historical Division, Headquarters, United States Army, Europe. Also used are Department of the Army pamphlets, at least partially based on the same sources. In the footnotes these sources are cited by the following alphanumeric designations:

Department of the Army pamphlets:

DA PAM 20—201	*Military Improvisations During the Russian Campaign,* Washington, D.C., August 1951.
DA PAM 20—269	*Small Unit Actions During the German Campaign in Russia,* Washington, D.C., July 1953.
DA PAM 20—291	*Effects of Climate on Combat in European Russia,* Washington, D.C., February 1952.
DA PAM 20—292	*Warfare in the Far North,* Washington, D.C., October 1951.

Foreign Military Studies, Historical Division, Headquarters, United States Army, Europe:

MS D—266	"Combat in the East. Experiences of German Tactical and Logistical Units in Russia," mimeographed, *Foreign Military Studies*, vol. 1, no. 10, April 1952.
MS C—034	General der Infanterie Gustav Hoehne, "In Snow and Mud: 31 Days of Attack Under Seydlitz During Early Spring of 1942," 20 October 1948.
MS D—020	Generaloberst Dr. Lothar Rendulic, "Field Expedients," 23 February 1947.
MS D—035	_____. "Effect of Extreme Cold on Weapons, Wheeled Vehicles, and Track Vehicles," 24 February 1947.

MS D—078	General der Infanterie Otto Schellert, "Winter Fighting of the 253rd Infantry Division in the Rzhev Area in 1941—42," draft translation reproduced by the Office of the Chief of Military History, Department of the Army, Washington, D.C., 1952.
MS D—106	Generaloberst Dr. Lothar Rendulic, "Combat in Deep Snow," 19 April 1947.
MS D—184	Generalleutnant Walter Friedrich Poppe, "Winter Campaign 1941—42; Campaign of the 255th Infantry Division East and South of Temkino, Mid-December 1941 to April 1942 (Area of Army Group Center)," draft translation reproduced by the Office of the Chief of Military History, Department of the Army, Washington, D.C., 1953.
MS D—277	Generalmajor Karl Rein, "Regiment in the Attack Through Snow-Covered Primeval Forests January 1942," draft translation reproduced by the Office of the Chief of Military History, Department of the Army, Washington, D.C., 1952.
MS D—285	General der Artillerie Rudolf von Roman, "The 35th Infantry Division Between Moscow and Gzhatsk," draft translation reproduced by the Office of the Chief of Military History, Department of the Army, Washington, D.C., 1951 [assigned 1 April 1947].
MS P—062	Generalmajor Alfred Toppe, "Erfrierungsprobleme im deutschen Heer während des II. Weltkrieges" [Frostbite problems in the German Army during World War II], 22 February 1951.

[1]DA PAM 20—292, pp. 1—2.
[2]Kirill Meretskov, *Serving the People* (Moscow: Progress Publishers, 1971), p. 160.
[3]Marshal Georgii Zhukov, "The Battle of Moscow," in *Moscow 1941/1942 Stalingrad*, compiled by Vladimir Sevruk (Moscow: Progress Publishers, 1974), p. 53; Alfred W. Turney, *Disaster at Moscow: von Bock's Campaigns* (Albuquerque: University of New Mexico Press, 1970), p. 133.
[4]Turney, p. 133.
[5]Albert Seaton, *The Battle For Moscow 1941—1942* (New York: Stein and Day, 1971), p. 159.
[6]Zhukov in Sevruk, p. 53.
[7]Col. P. Zhilin, cited in John Erickson, *The Soviet High Command* (New York: St. Martin's Press, 1962), p. 641.
[8]For example, DA PAM 20—291, p. 5.
[9]Ibid., p. 4.
[10]Alexander [Aleksandr Alfredovich] Bek, *Volokolamsk Highway*, 2d rev. ed. (Moscow: Progress Publishers, 1969), p. 149.
[11]Seaton, pp. 214—17.
[12]MS C—034, p. 4.
[13]A. Emerenko, *The Arduous Beginning* (Moscow: Progress Publishers, 1966), p. 275.
[14]German General Lothar Rendulic noted that, because of a hiatus in heavy snowfall for several weeks before the end of January 1942, the snow on most of the roads used for operations had already been so well packed that movement was possible. He also observed, however, that the narrow confines of such packed areas enabled the enemy to concentrate firepower effectively. MS D—106, pp. 3, 10.
[15]MS D—184, p. 19. Soviet sources support that conclusion, for example, Marshal Rokossovsky, "Forward," *Soviet Military Review*, no. 12, December 1971, p. 37.
[16]MS C—034, p. 5.
[17]Seaton, pp. 38, 133, 134.

[18] Turney, p. 147.
[19] Seaton, p. 213.
[20] DA PAM 20–291, p. 18.
[21] Zhukov in Sevruk, p. 53.
[22] Turney, p. 139.
[23] Lt. R. J. H. Haynes, "Soviet Techniques in Winter Warfare," *Journal of the Royal United Services Institute for Defense Studies* 119, no. 2 (June 1974):59.
[24] Dr. Berthold Mikat, "Die Erfrierungen bei den Soldaten der deutschen Wehrmacht im letzten Weltkrieg" [Frostbite among the German armed forces in the last world war] in MS P–062, Anlage [appendix] 8, pp. 2, 4.
[25] Turney, p. 128.
[26] Seaton, p. 288.
[27] MS D–184, p. 20.
[28] MS D–285, p. 4.
[29] Meretskov, pp. 157, 160.
[30] DA PAM 20–269, pp. 15–18.
[31] Meretskov, pp. 160–61.
[32] Nikolai Amosoff, *PPG–2266: A Surgeon's War*, translated and adapted by George St. George (Chicago: Henry Regnery Co., 1975), p. 102.
[33] MS D–078, p. 17.
[34] DA PAM 20–291, pp. 21–22.
[35] MS D–277, p. 4.
[36] MS D–020, pp. 4–5.
[37] MS D–277, p. 4.
[38] DA PAM 20–201, pp. 52–53. It is essential to adopt the latest scientific improvements in winter clothing, shelter, transport, and weaponry, but in the stark reality of the battlefield the most sophisticated equipment is apt to break down in unforeseen circumstances. When that happens, it is often wise to imitate the simple customs of the local natives whose ancestors have adapted their ways to their environment for centuries. Western society has become so dependent on modern technology that one may well wonder how many of today's generation would know which end of a *panje* horse to harness.
[39] MS D–285, p. 18.
[40] B. H. Liddell Hart, ed., *The Red Army* (New York: Harcourt, Brace and Co., 1956), pp. 337–42.
[41] DA PAM 20–291, p. 11.
[42] DA PAM 20–292, p. 16.
[43] DA PAM 20–291, p. 12.
[44] Seaton, p. 255.
[45] Ibid., p. 163.
[46] DA PAM 20–291, pp. 16–17.
[47] Ibid., p. 17.
[48] Meretskov, p. 190.
[49] DA PAM 20–291, p. 12.
[50] MS D–184, p. 5.
[51] MS D–277, p. 9.
[52] MS D–184, p. 15.
[53] MS D–035.
[54] DA PAM 20–291, p. 4.
[55] MS D–285, p. 3.
[56] DA PAM 20–291, pp. 5, 19.
[57] *Halder Diaries*, 6 December 1941 entry.
[58] DA PAM 20–269, pp. 27–28.
[59] DA PAM 20–291, p. 69.
[60] MS D–035.
[61] DA PAM 20–291, p. 19.
[62] MS D–035.
[63] MS C–034, pp. 12, 19–20.

[64] MS B—266, p. 44.
[65] MS D—035.
[66] DA PAM 20—291, p. 19.
[67] MS D—184, p. 6; MS D—285, p. 5.
[68] MS D—106, pp. 12—14.
[69] DA PAM 20—201, p. 24.
[70] DA PAM 20—291, p. 5.
[71] Lieutenant General Sir Mason-MacFarlane, "Russian Artillery 1941—45," *The Journal of the Royal Artillery* 74, no. 4 (October 1947):326.
[72] DA PAM 20—201, pp. 23—24.
[73] MS D—277, p. 8. The Soviet Army has since perfected systematic blasting patterns for individual foxholes, bunkers, trenches, and gun and tank emplacements. See Haynes, pp. 60—62.
[74] MS D—020, p. 6.
[75] DA PAM 20—269, pp. 22—23.
[76] "Winter Experiences of the German Air Force Ground Units," translated and digested in *Military Review* 29, no. 7 (October 1949):85.

☆ U.S. Government Printing Office: 1982—564-005/2025 Region No. 6

www.ingramcontent.com/pod-product-compliance
Lightning Source LLC
Chambersburg PA
CBHW081329040426
42453CB00013B/2350